Teeline Dictation and Drill Book

I. C. HILL and G. S. HILL

Heinemann Educational Books
London

Heinemann Educational Books Ltd
22 Bedford Square, London WC1B 3HH.

LONDON EDINBURGH MELBOURNE AUCKLAND
HONG KONG SINGAPORE KUALA LUMPUR NEW DELHI
IBADAN NAIROBI JOHANNESBURG
EXETER (NH) KINGSTON PORT OF SPAIN

ISBN 0 435 45343 2

First published 1980
Reprinted 1982

British Library Cataloguing in Publication Data

Hill, Ivy Constance
   Teeline dictation and drill book.
   1. Shorthand – Teeline – Exercises for dictation
   I. Title   II. Hill, G
   653'.428   Z56
   ISBN 0-435-45343-2

Printed in Great Britain by
Biddles Ltd., Guildford, Surrey.

Contents

Writers and Teachers of Teeline

are invited to join

THE TEELINE ASSOCIATION LTD.

members of which receive the quarterly

magazine, TEELINE TIMES, free of charge.

For details and application forms write to:

The Membership Secretary,
The Teeline Association Ltd.,
c/o 128 Kent Road, (Registered Office)
Mapperley, Nottingham, NG3 6BS.

Introduction

A great many requests have been made by Teeline teachers over several years
for a dictation book.   It seems that dictation material is something of
which shorthand teachers can never have enough.   This book is an attempt
to meet that need.

This book, however, has not been written solely for the teacher.   A study
of it should benefit any writer who wishes to increase speed, and it could
also form the basis of a second-session study course or a speed class.

To obtain the maximum value from dictation material, it should be designed

1)   systematically to consolidate theory principles,

2)   to give sufficient repetition of the most commonly-used words and
        phrases to enable the writer, in due course, to respond automatically
        to them, and

3)   to present the kind of challenge which will be met with in subsequent
        examinations.

All the passages are marked in tens, thus allowing them to be read at any
speed and all are preceded by a Facility Drill which is composed mainly of
words and groupings NOT included in the Teeline textbook or workbooks.
These drills enable any student to prepare the passage, either for dictation
in class or (with several empty lines below each line of Teeline) for use
as a timed transcription exercise or, if there is no-one available to give
speed dictation, for a reading and copying drill.   Working through the
book in this way, should result in an overall increase in note-taking speed,
even if this cannot be measured as the study proceeds.

The first section of the book is linked to the textbook TEELINE.   Passages
in this section form a revision of theory and are, consequently, similar to
those in the textbook and First Teeline Workbook.

The second section is devoted to commercial material and mainly contains
longer passages for the building of stamina on topics which have particular
relevance to the secretarial or commercial student.   Letters can usually
be obtained easily from other sources and, for that reason, not many are
included.

The third section of general and journalistic material will be useful also
to non-journalists, and here there is a repetitive thread running through
the passages.

<u>The final section</u> gives a variety of material, mostly drawn from actual Teeline examination papers, which can be used for regular testing in preparation for the examination proper.

It is hoped that this book will thus help to supplement the teacher's own dictation material and fill a gap for the writer who, after completing the theory, cannot find a speed class to attend.

I. C. Hill and G. S. Hill.

Nottingham, 1980.

<u>GENERAL NOTES</u>

1. Dates and amounts of money are written out in words, to
    make numbering easier and to standardise the method of
    dictating, but writers are advised to transcribe these
    in figures, e.g.

        nineteen-forty-eight - 1948

        three-point-three million pounds - £3.3 million pounds.

2. The passages in Section 3 are examples of the kind of
    material journalists may be called upon to report. The
    authors wish to make it clear that the sentiments expressed
    are not their own and do not refer to any particular
    government or organisation, either in this country or
    overseas.

SECTION 1 : Graded Dictation

Before starting on this section, students are advised to read (or re-read)
the Notes to Students at the beginning of FIRST TEELINE WORKBOOK.

It is important when building speed, to cut out every unnecessary movement.
One way of doing this is to train yourself to group words where possible.
By joining two or more words together you save the time which would be needed
in moving your hand from one outline to the next.

By grouping, it is often possible too, to shorten the amount you need to write.
For instance, the word 'been' can be reduced to B only, the word 'have' to V
only and the word 'the' to H only.   These contracted forms can be used only
when the words are part of a grouping.

Chapter 4 in the textbook shows some simple word groupings.   The following
exercises may be studied once Page 30 has been reached.   It is suggested that
the following procedure is used:-

1. Copy the groupings given and drill them, preferably a few at a time
    working down the column, rather than one at a time across the page.

2. Put the passages into Teeline, using any of the groupings which appear
    in the lists and the outlines given in the Facility Drills, which precede
    each longhand passage.

3. Cover the passage (or close the book) and see if you can read or write
    it back from your Teeline notes.

4. Check your attempt from the book, paying particular attention to any word
    which presented difficulty or over which you made a mistake.

You are now ready to try taking the passage from dictation.   However, if you
have a special speed as your aim, you should re-read the passage from your
notes as many times as you need in order to read it in the same time as you
hope to take it down, e.g. if your aim is to take it down at 50 w.p.m., then
you should read your notes at 50 w.p.m. or over.   The more speed you can
achieve on the reading, the better chance you have of getting the piece down
from dictation.

Notice that the first word in a grouping sets the position, although where
the first word is followed by a T stroke, it may be written in the T position
to allow T to take its proper place in relation to the line, e.g. "as to that"
could be ⟨⟩ or ⟨⟩ .

<u>Study and practise these groupings</u>:-

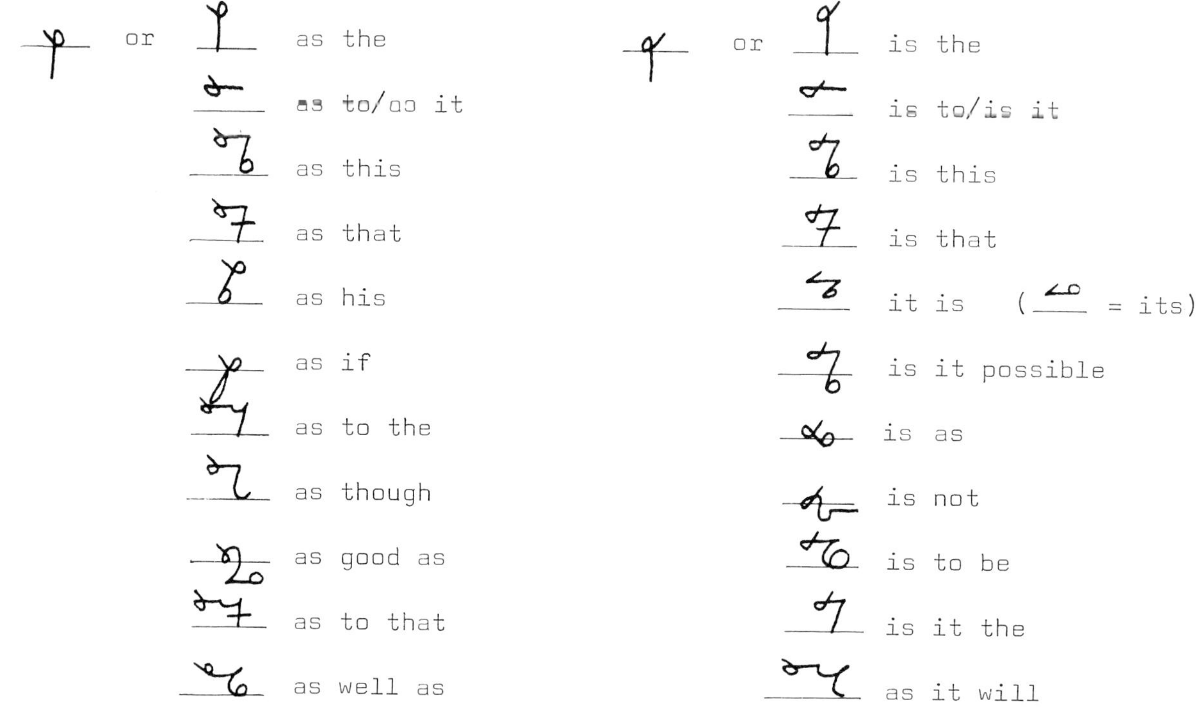

FACILITY DRILL 1:

don't   outside   (_____ = outset)   chance

or   quickly   usually   listen

anything   television   idle

something   lengthen   or   radio

PASSAGE 1:

As the days lengthen, we spend less time outside and [10] find things to do in the house. You may not [20] like having to stay in as much as being able [30] to get out, but I find this gives me a [40] chance to do all the jobs I don't do when [50] the nights are light and I am tempted to go [60] out. I get on with reading, sewing, baking and writing [70] and the nights pass very quickly. There is usually something [80] to listen to on the radio and something to watch [90] on the television.

<u>102 words</u>

<u>Practise these groupings</u>:   <u>HAVE</u>

you have   we have   have you   have we

have had   have not   haven't   may have

will have   would have   <u>NOTE</u>: Keep U & ⌣ distinct.

Keep U & V distinct.

<u>THAT</u>

that have   that this   that is   that is not

that is the   that it is   that would   that may be

<u>FACILITY DRILL 2</u>:

or   shortly   carried out   nowhere   nowhere else

hold the   meetings   buses

<u>PASSAGE 2</u>:

We have been told that-we may-have to give ^{10} up going to the Club shortly, because the hall we ^{20} use is to be closed while repairs are carried out ^{30} there. That is not good news, as we have nowhere ^{40} else to hold the meetings. There is a hall at ^{50} Long Lane but that would be difficult to reach as ^{60} the buses do not pass close enough to it.   We ^{70} may have to meet at my house until the repairs ^{80} are finished.   <u>82 words</u>

————————

<u>Practise these groupings</u>: <u>WITH</u>

with the   with this   with them   with these

with those   with its   with which   with which the

<u>OF</u>

of the   of this   of his   of these

of those   of which

<u>NOTICE</u> The need for control to distinguish between –
with which and of which, also have you and have we.

FACILITY DRILL 3:

____ upset ____ we are ____ or ____ someone

____ spoke ____ or ____ appears ____ us ____ this is the

PASSAGE 3:

This is the boy I spoke to you about. We $\overset{10}{/}$ are going with him to ask which of his teachers $\overset{20}{/}$ saw the rest of the class leave, as someone appears $\overset{30}{/}$ to have gone home with his coat by mistake. He $\overset{40}{/}$ is very upset about it, because it was quite a $\overset{50}{/}$ good coat. He had not had it very long, so $\overset{60}{/}$ we hope we shall be able to help him to $\overset{70}{/}$ find it.   72 words

HINT 1: Taking down continuous matter is more difficult than taking down one word at a time. This is because three things are happening all at the same time. You are hearing the words being dictated, but while you are writing them down you must also listen to what is being said and store it up in your memory until you have written it down. So, you are listening, writing and remembering all at once. This is a very complicated process and it may take you some time to master it. If you get too far behind the speaker - and you will have to be a little way behind to be able to make use of groupings - and forget what has been said, leave a gap in your notes and continue taking down the words being said at that moment. When you check your dictation, count up how many words you left out. It will probably be less than you imagined.

        You may also find that occasionally your mind goes quite blank, and you cannot remember what you have just heard. This may be because you are trying to work out a new or unusual word. When this happens, ignore what you have missed and pick up the dictation from that moment, checking at the end not only what you missed out but why you stopped when you did. If it was because of one word, practise it before trying that dictation again, so that it does not stop you next time.

Practise these groupings: OMISSION OF TO or T:

____ that is (to) say   ____ that is not (to) say

____ I mus(t) (s)ay   ____ I mus(t) not   ____ to (t)he

____ to (t)hat   ____ as to (t)hat   ____ needless (to) say

____

FACILITY DRILL 4:

____ which you have   ____ or ____ from the ____ from them

____ from me   ____ from him   ____ from his

PASSAGE 4:

Have you heard from the manager if the job which 10 you have been asking about is likely to be open 20 to you?   I must say it would be a step 30 up if you got it, but maybe it will go 40 to that young man who joined the staff last year. 50   Many seem to think he has a good chance of 60 it, and from his attitude and what he says, he seems 70 to think so too, but that is not to say 80 he will be the lucky one.   <u>86 words</u>

<u>Practise the following groupings</u>:   <u>BE/BEEN</u>   (In all cases, B may be reduced to the circle only if preferred.)

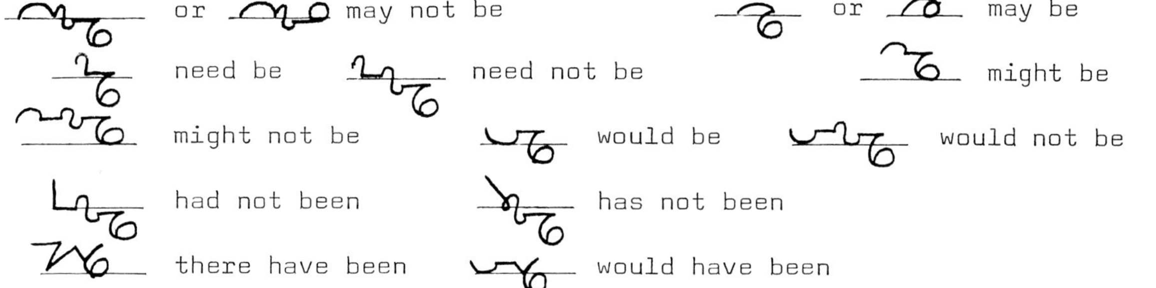

PASSAGE 5:

It would be a good idea if we had the 10 house painted before the end of the year.   It need 20 not cost a lot if we do it instead of 30 getting the usual man in.   It has not been painted 40 since we went to Italy, and that must be at 50 least five years ago.   I suggest that we have a 60 look at the latest shade card and see what will 70 be the best paint to get.   Then we will have 80 to decide just how we are going to do the 90 job and get on with it very soon.   <u>98 words</u>

<u>Revision Exercise 1</u>: (After Page 37)   <u>Put the following words into Teeline</u>:-
hanger,   language,   string,   strong,   stronger,   single,   swing, swinging,   strongly,   strength,   strengthen,   tongue,   knowingly, unknowingly,   bearings,   beginnings,   buildings,   fittings,   lining, blank,   shrinking,   trunk,   Frank,   feelingly,   drawing,   offering, feelings,   drunk.   (<u>Key on Page K1.</u>)

FACILITY DRILL 6:

without   petrol   fuming   accept

PASSAGE 6:

If I drew all my savings out of the building /[10] society I still would not be able to afford to /[20] buy a car, and it would be quite useless having /[30] a car if I had no money to pay for /[40] petrol and repairs.   Imagine my feelings if I had to /[50] leave it in the garage all the time.   But there /[60] is no point in fuming about it.   I may as /[70] well accept things cheerfully.   I would rather leave my shrinking /[80] savings where they are and know I have something to /[90] fall back on than buy something which I can manage /[100] very well without.

103 words

HINT 2:

When taking dictation be alert but not tense.   Sit comfortably, and use a firm working surface which is not too high for you.   Don't take dictation with your notebook balanced on your knee.   You may have to do this occasionall when you start work, but it is not a good way to practise.   Sit a little way away from the table or desk, with your back supported.   Leaning heavily on you arm or dropping your head over your book will quickly tire you, and gripping your pen tightly will tense your hand and arm muscles and make writing more difficult.

FACILITY DRILL 7:

✗ accident   ✗ or ✗ accidents   ⌐ avoided

snapped   or   narrowly.

PASSAGE 7:

Some strong language was used when a swinging door narrowly /[10] missed hitting one of the builders.   It should of course, /[20] not have been left open when there was a strong /[30] gusty wind blowing.   It was being held firm by a /[40] length of string, but this had snapped.   At the time /[50] the man was carrying a load of sand and if /[60] the door had caught this he could have been badly /[70] hurt.   Many accidents could be avoided with a little care. /[80]   80 words

Make sure you are writing O and U clearly.   Keep O a shallow curve and U a full one.   Practise these words.

opera   uproar   open   upon   onion   union

operate   upright   opposite/opposed   upset/upside

Copy them without writing the longhand, or take them down from dictation.
Then see if you can transcribe them correctly without referring to this
page until you have finished.

Make sure you are writing A and I in their proper directions. Practise:-

ice   ace   item   atom   Ida   Ada   in   an

If your outlines are correctly written and if you can develop a controlled
style of writing, you will find it easier to read back your notes quickly
and accurately.

FACILITY DRILL 8:   (To follow TR/TN blends)

strikes   district   loyalty   disruption

certain   danger   threatened

or   militant   or   refusing   trucks

I think that   thanked   thank you   my thanks

many thanks   tremendous

PASSAGE 8:

As most of you know, during the past few weeks /[10]there have been many strikes
in this district.   I think /[20]that the staff of this firm should be thanked
for /[30]their loyalty to us.   Not one day has been lost /[40]here by such
disruption.   So, I should like to begin /[50]this meeting by saying "Thank you
for your loyalty and /[60]good sense".   My thanks are also due to the drivers /[70]
who kept goods moving, in spite of tremendous difficulties and, /[80]in some
cases, a certain amount of danger from outside /[90]when they were threatened
by a militant few for refusing /[100]to leave their trucks.   104 words

Revision Exercise 2:   Put the following words into Teeline:-
                       (Words ending in T/D and D/D.)

accepted, deposited, studied, adapted, doubted, adjusted, hesitated, posted,

admitted, illustrated, repeated, asserted, listed, headed. (Key on Page K1.)

FACILITY DRILL 9:

editorial   union   members

whether or not   question   important

PASSAGE 9a:

The girl admitted that she had forgotten to post the [10] letter which her boss had said was important. When the [20] question was first put to her, she had hesitated, but [30] when it was repeated, she accepted that she was at [40] fault. She said that as she was going across the [50] road to put it into the box, two cars had [60] collided a few yards away. There was so much happening [70] during the following few minutes, that she had quite forgotten [80] about the letter, which she had slipped into her handbag. [90] It was still there.   94 words

PASSAGE 9b:

The editorial in that day's paper asserted that the Union [10] had not accepted the terms put to them by the [20] firm, but that its leaders would study the items listed [30] and advise their members whether or not to accept them. [40] This, said the writer, illustrated the need for a postal [50] ballot.   51 words

Revision Exercise 3: (Words containing NT/ND):

Put these words into Teeline:- absent, client, guarantee, joint, parents, rental, talent, calendar, cylinder, friendly, outlined, sandals, fastened, trained.   (Key on Page K1.)

FACILITY DRILL 10: Distinguishing Outlines:-

behind   beyond   or   equally   account

heating   (heading   )

PASSAGE 10:

My parents have a joint bank account. This is useful [10] for paying bills for such items as television rental, heating [20] and rates, which are necessary, and which are shared. But [30] it is not so easy regarding personal spending. While they [40] are on friendly terms, father is not likely to object [50] if mother buys a pair of sandals which she does [60] not really need, but there is no guarantee that they [70] will stay on friendly terms if one thinks that the [80] other is spending money wastefully. A joint bank account has [90] its uses, but it is often a good thing for [100] each parent to have a personal account also.

108 words

To follow Page 39 – Words using CON/COM/CT. – Practise:-

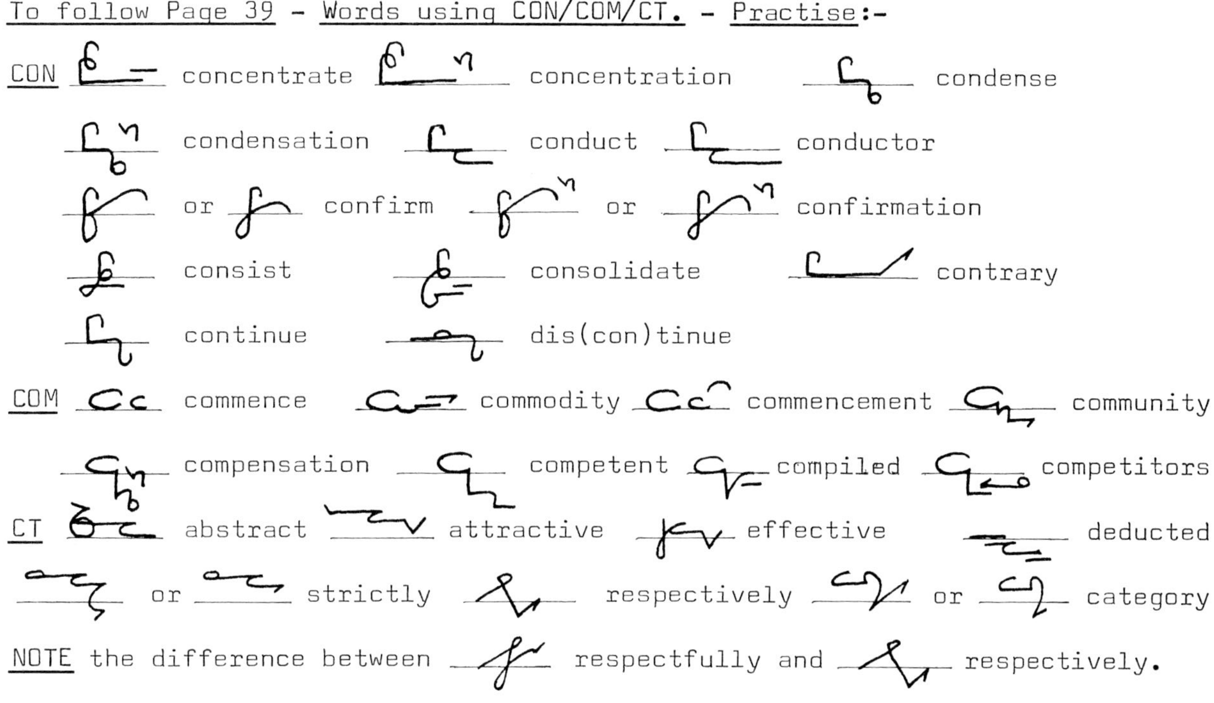

CON ___ concentrate ___ concentration ___ condense

___ condensation ___ conduct ___ conductor

___ or ___ confirm ___ or ___ confirmation

___ consist ___ consolidate ___ contrary

___ continue ___ dis(con)tinue

COM ___ commence ___ commodity ___ commencement ___ community

___ compensation ___ competent ___ compiled ___ competitors

CT ___ abstract ___ attractive ___ effective ___ deducted

___ or ___ strictly ___ respectively ___ or ___ category

NOTE the difference between ___ respectfully and ___ respectively.

Hint 3: If you make a mistake in taking down notes, never waste time in
rubbing out. Quickly cross out the wrong outline and then carry on.

        Don't worry if you fall behind the reader. Each time you attempt a
dictation, aim to get more down and to write the outlines more accurately on
each attempt. You will improve with practice. Not many people can take
everything down on the first attempt.

FACILITY DRILL 11:

___ favourite (note: ___ favoured) ___ enjoyment ___ England

___ fortunate ___ altogether ___ therefore ___ distances

___ long-distance ___ destination ___ children ___ family

___ journey ___ exciting ___ City (of) York ___ studied

___ Queen Victoria

PASSAGE 11:

Travelling by train is still the favourite form of transport ^{10} for many, and
train spotting offers a day's enjoyment to ^{20} small boys and to some who are
not so ^{30} young. In England today, we are fortunate enough to have ^{40} a very
good railway service, although there are some districts ^{50} which are not so

well served as they might be. ^{60} In some countries, trains are either few in number, or ^{70} lacking altogether, and one must, therefore, drive long distances by ^{80} road, travel by long-distance coach, or fly from one ^{90} destination to another. Many young children today, used to the ^{100} family car, find a journey by train both strange and ^{110} exciting, but years ago, it was just the opposite. Then, ^{120} few families had cars and if they had to travel ^{130} a long way it would usually be by train. The ^{140} City of York has a famous Railway Museum, where the ^{150} history of the railways may be studied. Queen Victoria liked ^{160} to travel by train and some of the carriages which ^{170} she used in those far-off days, are on show ^{180} there. <u>181 words</u>

FACILITY DRILL 12:

otherwise ____ particular ____ or ____ fortunately ____ skill ____ intense ____ mastered ____ worthwhile ____ achieved ____ on (the) other hand ____ or ____ shorthand ____ changed thing

PASSAGE 12a:

Dear Sir or Madam,

    We enclose a catalogue and price ^{10} list showing some of the most attractive lines which we ^{20} are able to offer to you at bargain prices. Some ^{30} are cheap simply because we intend to discontinue these particular ^{40} lines, and others, because they are very slightly damaged.

    As ^{50} these are sale items, we offer them on strictly cash ^{60} terms. Payment should be enclosed with your order. We are ^{70} sure you will find these goods better value than anything ^{80} you will be able to purchase from our competitors at ^{90} the same price. Hurry, while stocks last. Many of these ^{100} offers cannot be repeated.

Yours truly. <u>106 words</u>

PASSAGE 12b:

Those who have talent should make every effort to see ^{10} that they are trained to make the best use of ^{20} it, otherwise they may not become effective operators in their ^{30} particular field. Many commence their training cheerfully enough, but discontinue ^{40} their studies before they are fully competent. Some skills, demand [50] intense concentration on the part of the student before success [60] is achieved, but once the skill is mastered, it all [70] seems worthwhile. On the other hand, if the skill is [80] not mastered, then all the time and effort will have [90] been wasted. Shorthand writing falls into this category, but fortunately, [100] Teeline has changed things for many who had failed at [110] other kinds of shorthand.   114 words

FACILITY DRILL 13: Practise: (to follow the N blends – Chapter 6 textbook)

amongst   amongst their   charity   or   appeal

starving   P.D.S.A.   rubbish

PASSAGE 13:

It is wonderful to find someone who can think of [10] a use for some of the unwanted things we all [20] have in the house. I heard the other day on [30] the radio, that two children had found so many unwanted [40] items amongst their toys and books that they had been [50] able to raise a considerable sum of money for a [60] charity appeal to help starving children in another country. I [70] am always glad to see the P.D.S.A. [80] van come round, as then I can get rid of [90] my own particular rubbish. I suppose this is why there [100] are so many 'nearly-new' shops nowadays. What one person [110] considers to be rubbish, another person is happy to own. [120]   120 words

(NOTE: P.D.S.A. = People's Dispensary for Sick Animals)

FACILITY DRILL 14:   unknown   enthusiastically   bounce

sound   drowning   supporters   trench

bounced   drowned   referee   annoyance

PASSAGE 14:

When the ball hit the post and bounced back after [10] the home side's attempt to score a goal, the supporters [20] roared their annoyance, while the visitors cheered enthusiastically. The sound [30] of the referee's whistle was almost drowned by the volume [40] of noise. It is said that the violence sometimes shown [50] by football fans against rival supporters is unknown at rugger [60] matches, although the latter sport is rough and the spectators [70] make just as much noise. I wonder why this is. [80]   80 words

FACILITY DRILL 15: (to follow the X blends - Page 44 textbook)

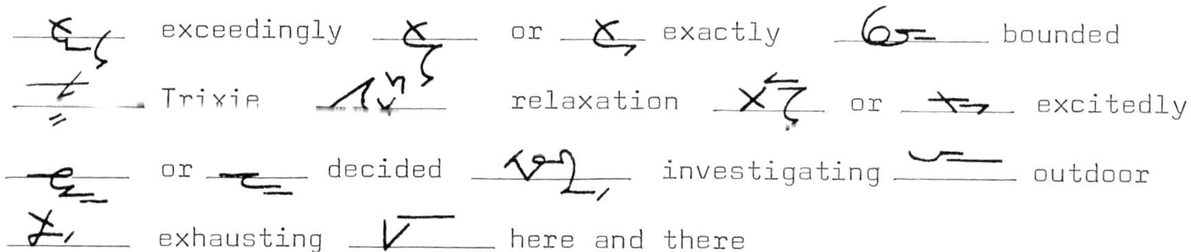

exceedingly   or   exactly   bounded

Trixie   relaxation   or   excitedly

or   decided   investigating   outdoor

exhausting   here and there

PASSAGE 15:

It was exactly a quarter past six when Trixie took 10 the dog for his usual walk. He bounded along in 20 front of her, excitedly tugging at his lead for so 30 long, then coming to a sudden stop as he decided 40 that something here or there needed investigating. These stoppings and 50 startings tended to make the walk rather exhausting and also 60 to extend the time it took, but as Trixie had 70 nothing better to do, she did not mind much. Taking 80 the dog for a walk was a form of relaxation 90 which cost nothing and which gave her good outdoor exercise. 100

100 words

FACILITY DRILL 16:

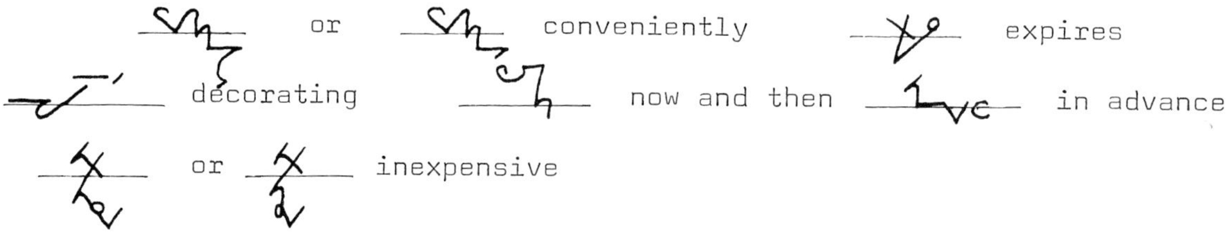

or   conveniently   expires

decorating   now and then   in advance

or   inexpensive

PASSAGE 16:

The lease on this luxury flat expires at the end 10 of next month. I am not altogether sorry, as it 20 is very expensive and needs decorating. I am looking for 30 something conveniently near the office and should like an extra 40 room so that I can invite friends to stay now 50 and then. If you hear of anything suitable, I should 60 be glad to know. Inexpensive flats in good districts are 70 hard to come by in this town and owners are 80 often unwilling to let them unless they can get at 90 least a month's rent in advance. I could afford that. 100

100 words

FACILITY DRILL 17a: (to follow Page 46, textbook)

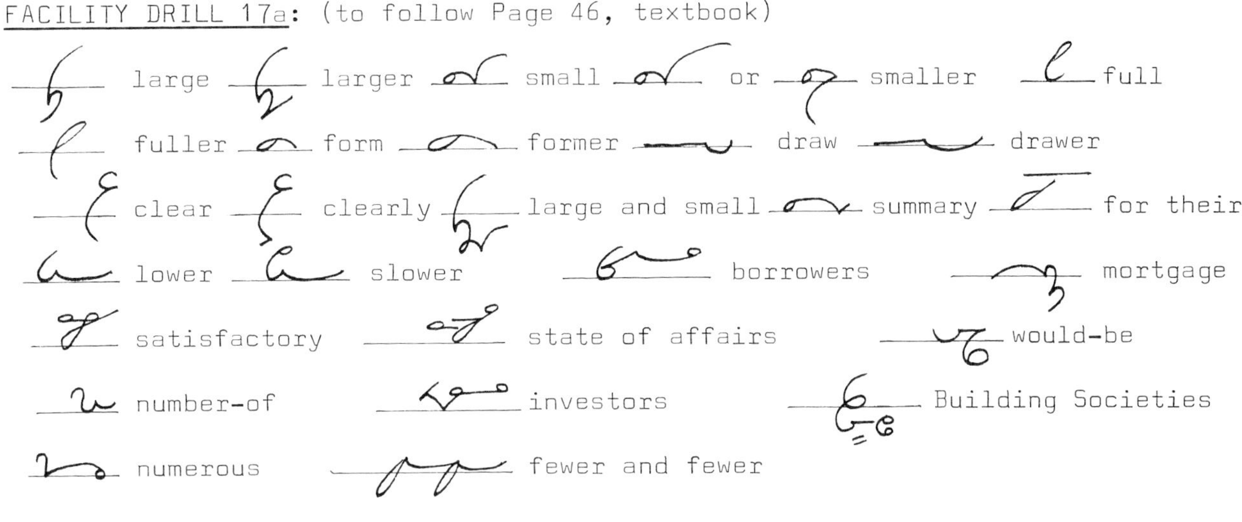

large   larger   small   or   smaller   full
fuller   form   former   draw   drawer
clear   clearly   large and small   summary   for their
lower   slower   borrowers   mortgage
satisfactory   state of affairs   would-be
number-of   investors   Building Societies
numerous   fewer and fewer

NOTE: Do not be afraid of lengthening the LR, MR & WR strokes. They will
        then be easier to read back quickly because they will be distinct
        from ordinary L, M & W.

PASSAGE 17a:

The current shortage of funds held by the Building Societies $\frac{10}{}$ means that
the number of borrowers this year is lower $\frac{20}{}$ than it was last year, and
unless many more investors $\frac{30}{}$ deposit their money in this particular area,
fewer and fewer would-be home buyers will be able to obtain the $\frac{50}{}$ necessary
mortgage. Clearly, this is a far from satisfactory state $\frac{60}{}$ of affairs.

62 words

FACILITY DRILL 17b:

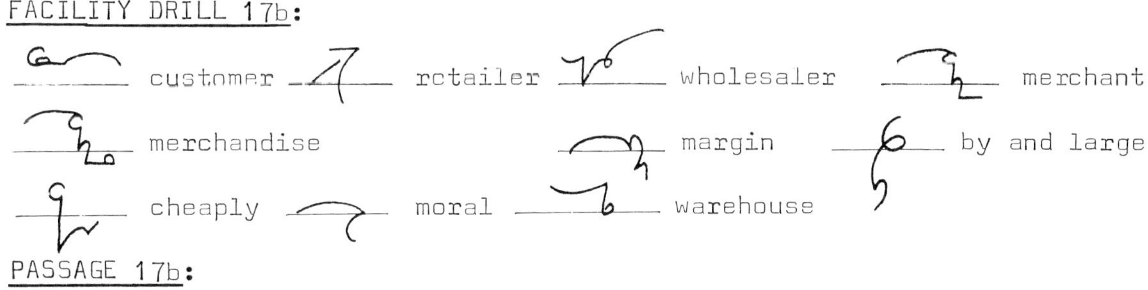

customer   retailer   wholesaler   merchant
merchandise   margin   by and large
cheaply   moral   warehouse

PASSAGE 17b:

It is clear that if goods pass through many hands $\frac{10}{}$ before reaching the
customer, the more the price of them $\frac{20}{}$ will rise, as the merchant, the
wholesaler and the retailer $\frac{30}{}$ all have to make a little on the exchange.
The / moral of this then, is that, by and large, the $\frac{40}{}$ fewer the number
handling the merchandise, the lower the price $\frac{50}{}$ is likely to be. Those
customers who can go direct $\frac{70}{}$ to the warehouse for their goods, usually buy
them more $\frac{80}{}$ cheaply than they can in the shops.

87 words

<u>FACILITY DRILL 18</u>: (to follow Page 48, textbook)

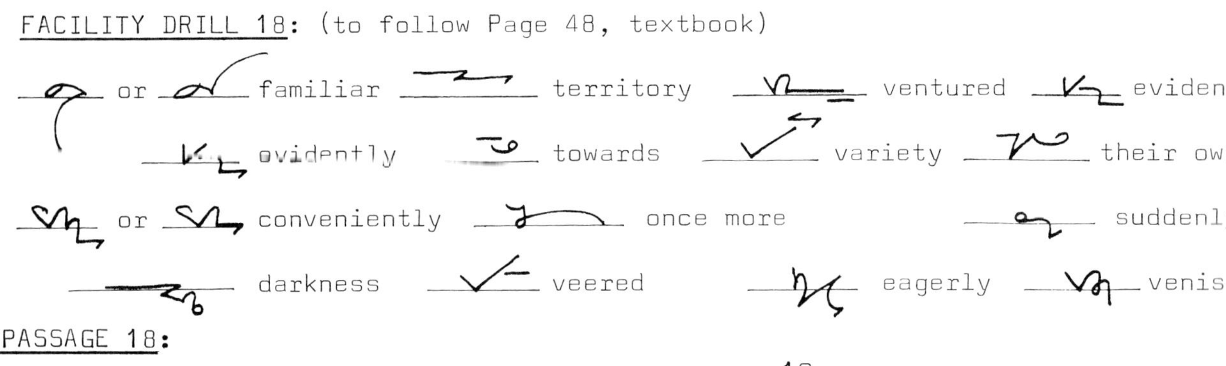

<u>PASSAGE 18</u>:

They ventured to the edge of the clearing and saw /10 that once more they had con
back into their own 20/ territory.   As they walked on, a variety of familiar
sounds 30/ came to them and it was evident that they were /40 quite near to the ca
This was most convenient, as 50/ the evening was at hand and soon darkness would
be 60/ upon them.   Suddenly, the smell of venison stew reached them /70 and,
picking up the scent, they veered eagerly towards it. 80/   <u>80 words</u>

<u>HINT 4</u>: Whenever you have to leave a gap in your notes, try to discover if it
was because you hesitated over one word.   Practise such words, so that next
time you will not hesitate when you hear them.

Avoid leaving large gaps between outlines, as this takes up valuable
space and time. Every movement which does not result in an outline going down
is wasting time. Write each outline as near to the next as if you were writin
in ordinary longhand. Making use of word groupings and abbreviated outlines
helps you to write more quickly than if you write each word separately and in
full.

<u>PASSAGE 19</u>:

When families go on holiday, they hope the weather will /10 be kind to them as
they usually wish to spend 20/ quite a lot of time out of doors.   This, of 30/
course, does not always happen, so it is wise to 40/ choose somewhere where ther
are things to do if it 50/ does rain, otherwise the holiday will be wasted.   It
is 60/ of little use being on a farm, miles from the 70/ nearest town, if it is
going to be too wet 80/ to get out much of the time. On the other 90/ hand, the
whole idea of taking a holiday in the 100/ country should be to get away from
traffic and shops. 110/   <u>110 words</u>

<u>FACILITY DRILL 20</u>:   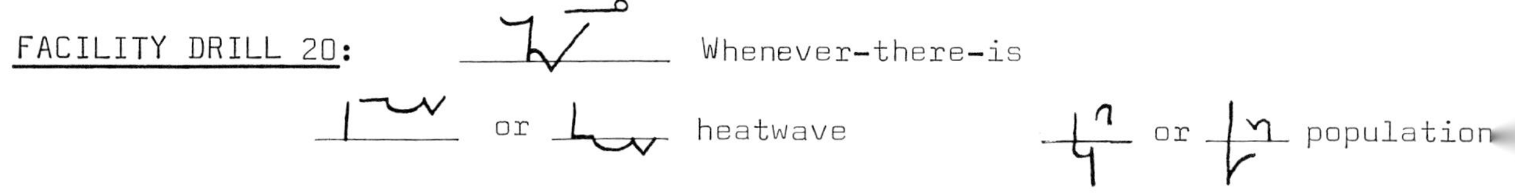

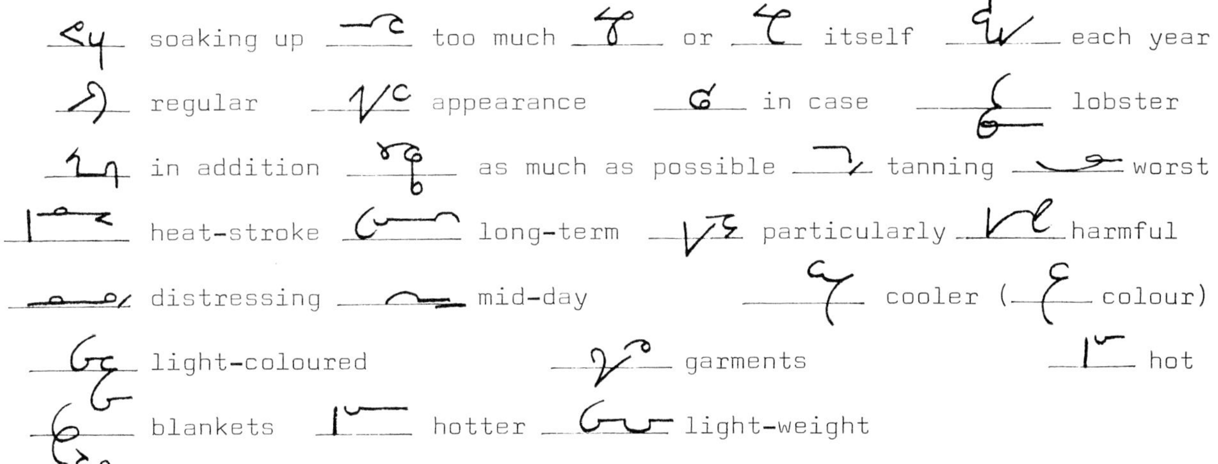

PASSAGE 20:

Whenever there is a heat-wave in England, half the [10] population makes itself ill by soaking up too much sun [20] in too little time. I suppose if we knew that [30] for several months in each year, we could be sure [40] of regular sunny days, we should not be so silly, [50] but there is a feeling that we must make the [60] most of the sun when it appears, in case that [70] is all we are going to see of it for [80] the rest of the year. It adds nothing to a [90] person's attractiveness to look like a boiled lobster and, in [100] addition, it is fairly dangerous to burn the skin. Medical [110] opinion nowadays is that one should keep out of the [120] sun as much as possible. At best, tanning simply ages [130] the skin, once the tan has faded. At the worst, [140] a person could suffer from heat-stroke or long-term [150] skin damage.

It is particularly distressing to see babies and [160] young children exposed to the rays of the mid-day [170] sun, without some covering on their heads. The rays of [180] the evening sun are not harmful and this is the [190] time to enjoy sitting or working outside without the worry [200] of any bad effects from too much sun-worship.

Those [210] who live in hot countries have more sense than [220] we have. They know that it is cooler to cover the [230] body with light-coloured, light-weight garments than to throw [240] off as much as possible. In fact, those who dwell [250] in hot desert regions, often wear heavy clothing like blankets [260] to keep out the heat of the sun which would [270] only make them hotter than they already are.

278 words

NOTE WARY and WEARY could be misread, e.g. He was a little wary of such
     questions. He was a little weary of such questions.

As WARY is the less common of the two words, vocalise it - WARY ⌣ WEARY ⌣

Be on the look-out for similar pairs of words, and decide which one you will
vocalise. (See Note on Page 18.)

FACILITY DRILL 21: (to follow Page 50)

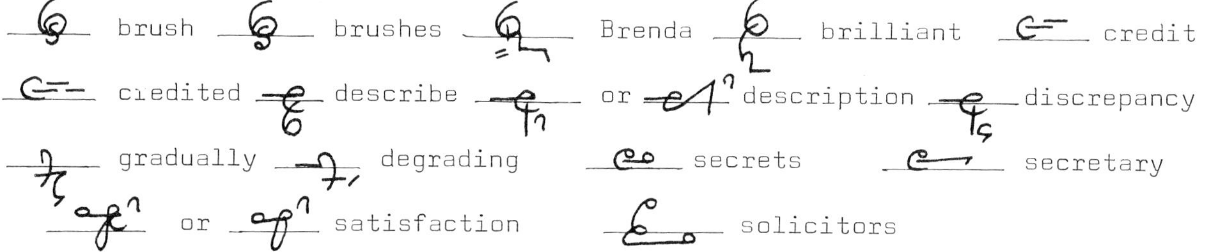

PASSAGE 21a:

Brenda could not have been described as a brilliant student ^{10}but, to her cred
once she had begun a job ^{20}she had the determination not to give up until it ^{3}
was finished to her own satisfaction. So, when she decided ^{40}to train as a
secretary, she worked very hard to ^{50}master the necessary skills, and graduall
she achieved her goal. ^{60} She is now working for a firm of solicitors in ^{70}
the city, and finding it is a very interesting job. ^{80} 80 words

PASSAGE 21b:

Dear Sir, We are sorry it has been necessary for ^{10}you to write to us about
the discrepancy in the ^{20}bill we sent you last week for the set of ^{30}brushes
which you purchased from us. As the sum involved ^{40}is so small, it will be
easier for us if ^{50}you will agree to accept a cash refund. We enclose ^{60}a
credit note, which you can change at this office ^{70}next time you are in town.
If this is not ^{80}convenient, however, the amount can be credited against a
future purchase from any of our shops. Yours truly.   98 words

FACILITY DRILL 22: (to follow Page 52)

    proceed   procedure   process   procession

    processed   processes   processing   prospers

    or   proprietor   promotion   profession   prosperous

_|\|_ proven _m_ prominent _|v_ professional _p_ prompt

_|h_ print-out _||_ pre-packed _|v_ proved _&_ beforehand

_|s_ appreciation _ub_ qualifications _h_ at the beginning

_%_ T.B.

<u>NOTE</u>: <u>Distinguishing Outlines</u>: _/_ prior _//_ priority

_/w_ or _/_ personnel _/v_ personal

<u>PASSAGE 22a</u>:

Many women today are so used to having pre-packed 1^0 foods from which to prepare meals, that they would be 2^0 more than a little apprehensive if they had to start 3^0 from scratch. However, if their efforts were successful, I think 4^0 their families might prefer home cooking to something which had 5^0 come out of a packet or a tin. Fresh food 6^0 usually tastes better than the processed kind.

<u>67 words</u>

<u>PASSAGE 22b</u>:

Prevention is better than cure. This is one of many 1^0 old sayings which was popular at the beginning of the 2^0 century. In some cases, it has been proved to be 3^0 true. For example, an x-ray can show early signs 4^0 of disease, so that prompt and proper treatment can be 5^0 given and so improve the patient's chances of survival; while 6^0 better food and living conditions have almost wiped out T.B. 7^0 which used to cause many deaths prior to the First 8^0 World War.

<u>82 words</u>

<u>NOTE</u>: _C_ century, needs vocalising for each recognition. _C_ = country. Alternatively a large C can be used to denote century e.g. _(14)_ = 14th Century.

<u>PASSAGE 22c</u>:

The personnel officer studied the computer print-out which listed 1^0 the qualifications of those being considered for promotion. Priority had 2^0 been given to candidates with the right personal qualities, as 3^0 well as the required experience, and the final choice would 4^0 be made that afternoon by a board of prominent business 5^0 and professional men. It was important that everything was ready 6^0 for the meeting and that everyone knew the proper procedure 7^0 beforehand.

<u>71 words</u>

FACILITY DRILL 23 (to follow Page 55)

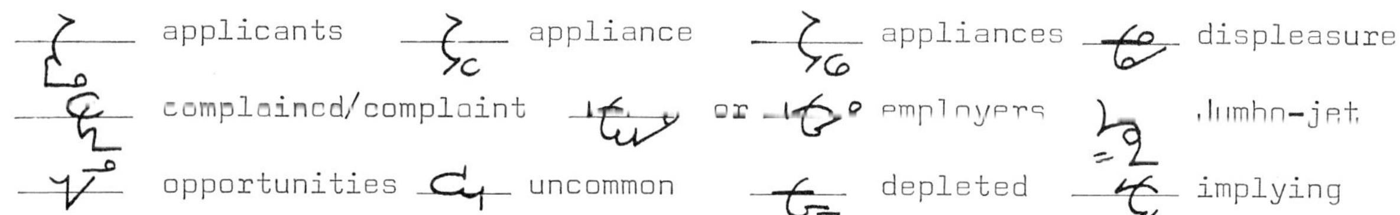

applicants   appliance   appliances   displeasure

complained/complaint   or   employers   Jumbo-jet

opportunities   uncommon   depleted   implying

PASSAGE 23a:

Several of the applicants complained that they were kept waiting /a long time before being interviewed and that no-one /explained why this was necessary. Naturally, they did not like /to express their displeasure at the time, but they felt /that their employers should now be made aware of their /complaints in case they had any explanation to offer. Some /people were implying that the interview had been arranged simply /to comply with the regulations.

<u>75 words</u>

PASSAGE 23b:

The ambassador was dispatched by Jumbo-jet to the newly-/formed republic to present his country's compliments to its leader, /as a symbol of support for the new regime and /to explore opportunities for trade between the two nations in /the future.

<u>42 words</u>

<u>NOTE</u>: Two other similar words are SIMPLE and SAMPLE, e.g. you could confuse a 'simple list' with a 'sample list', or a 'simple pattern' with a 'sample pattern'. Vocalise SIMPLE - keeping the unvocalised outline for SAMPLE - .

FACILITY DRILL 24: (to follow Page 57)

incentive   incident   incidentally   incorporated

inspect   inspector   insisted   instinct

instruct   instructor   absolute   failure

innocent

PASSAGE 24a:

If he felt that the evidence was incriminating, the inspector /was inclined to adopt an uncompromising attitude to the suspect /as if encouraging him to

confess his guilt, even though [30]the man insisted that he was innocent.
The inspector had [40]an uncommon instinct for detecting crime. He was,
incidentally, rarely [50]wrong.   51 words

PASSAGE 24b:

To be a successful instructor, it is necessary to encourage [10]those who are
being instructed; otherwise, they have little incentive [20]to keep on trying.
It is better to start by [30]telling the student what he is doing right and
then [40]to explain how he could improve, instead of telling him [50]that he is
doing the job incorrectly and omitting to [60]mention that he is not an
absolute failure.   68 words

FACILITY DRILL 25:   preferred   probably
          bakery   embroidery   instrument

PASSAGE 25:

During the bakery strikes of the past few years, many [10]people tried their
hands at making their own bread, and [20]discovered that they preferred it to
the bought variety.   Their [30]grandmothers would probably never have thought
of buying bread.   They [40]needed to live economically, and it was cheaper to
bake [50]bread at home.   A woman who could not turn out [60]good bread and
cakes was considered to be an incompetent [70]housewife.   Of course, the
better-off had servants to do [80]this work for them, so they became accomplished
in other [90]ways, such as playing a musical instrument or doing embroidery. [100]
                                                                 100 words

FACILITY DRILL 26:

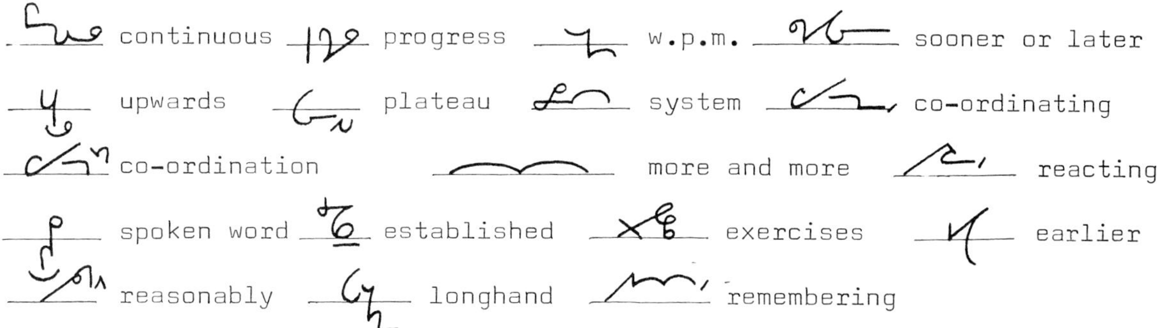

continuous   progress   w.p.m.   sooner or later
upwards   plateau   system   co-ordinating
co-ordination   more and more   reacting
spoken word   established   exercises   earlier
reasonably   longhand   remembering

PASSAGE 26:

Speed building is not a matter of making continuous progress. [10] It may take you some time to reach 40 w.p.m. [20] and then you may move fairly easily and [30] quickly to 50 or even 60 w.p.m., but [40] sooner or later you will reach what is called a [50] 'plateau'. You will stick on one speed level for so [60] long that you will begin to think you are never [70] going to improve and may decide to stop trying. This [80] is just the point at which you must keep on, [90] because if you feel you are actually getting worse instead [100] of better, you will be on the verge of reaching [110] a higher speed level. Eventually you will leave that plateau [120] and begin to climb upwards until the next plateau is [130] reached. It is necessary for you to understand that this [140] happens to everyone who learns a shorthand system, whatever the [150] system is, and it is connected with the processes we [160] have already described – co-ordinating your writing, thinking and remembering. [170] This co-ordination has to be done more and more [1] quickly as your speed increases and until new patterns of [190] reacting to the spoken word are established, you will seem [200] to make little or no progress. During these times, try [210] revising earlier exercises or reading through the theory again. Sometimes [220] reading your earlier notes as fast as you can will [2] help. Remember too, how long it took you to learn [240] to read and write ordinary longhand at a reasonable speed. [250]

<u>250 words</u>

FACILITY DRILL 27:

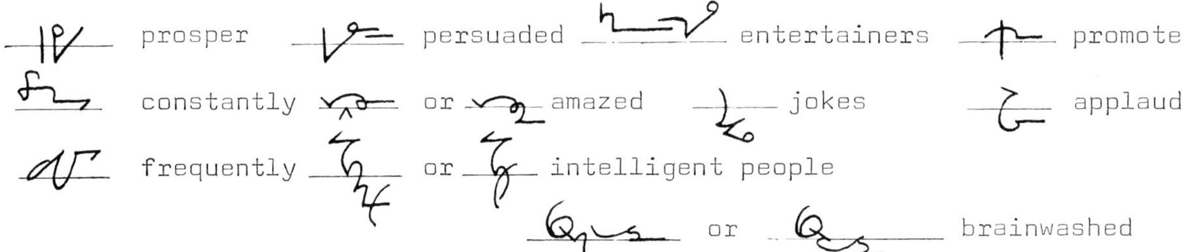

prosper   persuaded   entertainers   promote

constantly   or   amazed   jokes   applaud

frequently   or   intelligent people

or   brainwashed

PASSAGE 27:

No-one, it seems, can prosper today without publicity. New [10] products are put on the market only after intensive advertising [20] campaigns, and many people do not realise that they are [30] paying, not only for the product, but for being persuaded [40] to buy it. Entertainers have to pay an agent or [50] employ a publicity manager to promote them and find them [60] work. With enough publici-

even a poor actor or singer /70 can become famous. I am constantly amazed by the way /80 so many members of the public can laugh at jokes /90 which are not funny, applaud singers who cannot sing, and /100 generally appear to enjoy shows which are mainly rubbish, just /110 because they have been told frequently enough and loudly enough /120 that the people they are watching are good. How is /130 it that otherwise intelligent people can be so brainwashed by /140 the publicity machine?

143 words

FACILITY DRILL 28 (to follow Page 62)

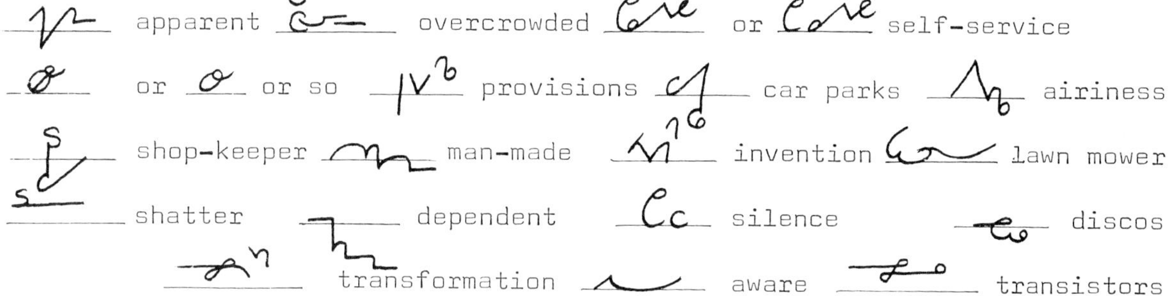

PASSAGE 28a:

In the aftermath of the Christmas holiday, I had to /10 go into town, and was surprised to find it as /20 crowded as it had been before Christmas. Both the underground /30 and multi-storey car parks were full. In the circumstances, /40 it was as well I had travelled by public transport. /50 The reason for the crowds became apparent when I looked /60 in the shop windows. It was sale time! I had /70 some business to transact at the bank, where I joined /80 a long queue. In fact, there were queues everywhere, so /90 I decided to get out of the over-crowded city /100 centre and leave the rest of my shopping until another /110 afternoon.

111 words

PASSAGE 28b:

The shops have undergone a transformation during the past twenty /10 or so years. Once, most people bought their provisions at /20 the local corner shops, where they were known to the /30 proprietor and where they could pay at the end of /40 the week if they were above suspicion. Now, most families /50 can afford to go to the supermarkets and pay cash. /60 Many like the self-service system, the wide range of /70 goods offered and the bright airiness of these places.   Others 7^{80} prefer to shop where they can get personal service and 7^{90} advice from the shop-keeper.   95 words.

PASSAGE 20c:

One of the main changes which has taken place in 7^{10} the world since I was a child is the multiplication 7^{20} of man-made noise.   Some of this comes from automobiles 7^{30} and aeroplanes, which were rarely seen or heard before the 7^{40} First World War, and some from the invention of tools 7^{50} which use electricity. The electric lawn mower and hedge cutter 7^{60} are two which spring to mind and which often shatter 7^{70} the peace of summer afternoons, while indoors one has the 7^{80} noise of radio, television, air-conditioning and so on.   The 7^{90} young grow up bathed in an everlasting tide of noise, 7^{100} so that they cease to be aware of it, and 7^{110} yet, at the same time, become dependent on it, for 7^{120} wherever they go, their transistors have to go too.   Silence, 7^{130} for them, is not golden.   Their discos throb with a 7^{140} level of sound which, to the older generation, is overpowering. 7^{150} 150 words

FACILITY DRILL 29: (to follow Page 69)

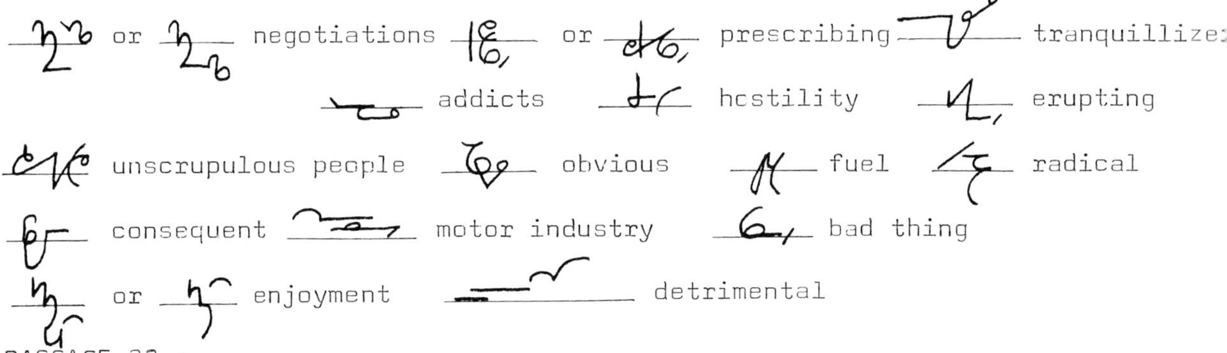

or   negotiations   or   prescribing   tranquillizer

addicts   hostility   erupting

unscrupulous people   obvious   fuel   radical

consequent   motor industry   bad thing

or   enjoyment   detrimental

PASSAGE 29a:

Negotiations have reached a crucial stage, and it is evident 7^{10} that a great deal of patience is going to be 7^{20} needed if a settlement is to be reached.   If the $7^{?}$ delicate balance of the talks is upset in any way, 7^{40} there is the danger of violence erupting, especially in the 7^{50} present climate of racial hostility. However, so long as all 7^{60} the parties involved can be kept round the table, there 7^{70} is hope that a way out of the troubles will 7^{80} be found.   82 words

PASSAGE 29b :

The problem of drug-taking is causing concern to many, including the police, sociologists and psychologists. Doctors have been blamed for prescribing too many tranquillizers and sleeping pills, which can have a detrimental effect upon their patients. But the root of the trouble lies in the fact that many young people take drugs as an experiment, for the excitement of it and because it is the fashionable thing to do, without realising the dangers involved. Because a good many unscrupulous people stand to make financial gain from the sale of drugs, it is difficult to control the spread of them, but until this is done, thousands will continue to die each year in misery, as a result of becoming drug addicts.   <u>121 words</u>

PASSAGE 29c:

Although it has been obvious to a few people for many years that the world's fuel supplies might dry up, only now are the majority beginning to realise that they may soon be forced to make radical alterations in their life-style. Cars have been getting more expensive and now the shortage of petrol is likely to mean a cut-back in the demand for them, with a consequent loss of jobs in the motor industry. In the long run, it may not be such a bad thing for the nation to have fewer vehicles on the road. Air pollution will be less, and having to walk more should keep people fitter and happier. Without a car, the average family would have more time and money to spend on other things, which would give them just as much enjoyment and less worry.   <u>144 words</u>

FACILITY DRILL 30 :

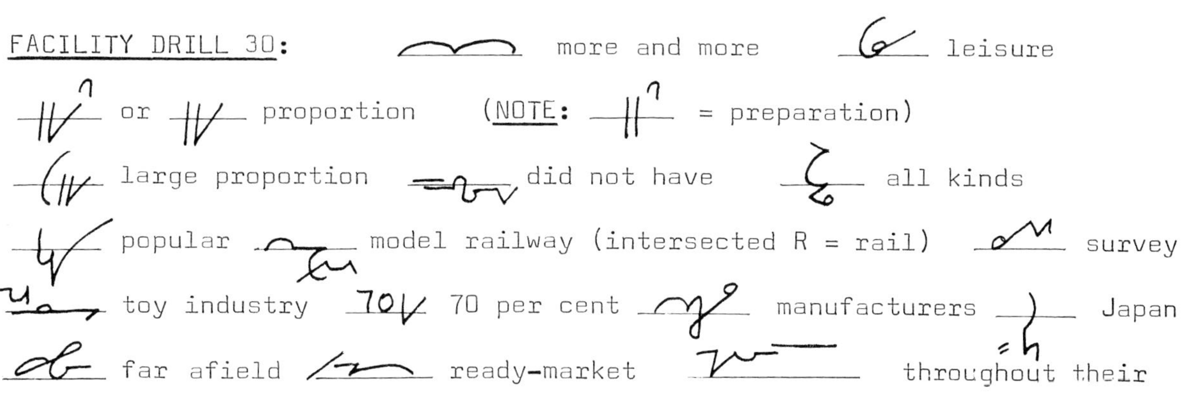

PASSAGE 30:

As more and more leisure time becomes available to a 10 large proportion of the working population in the U.K., working 20 men are reported to be spending their spare money on 30 the kind of toys they probably did not have when 40 they were children. Working models of all kinds are popular, 50 but the biggest sales are in the model railway section 60 of the toy industry. A recent survey suggests that 70 70 per cent of model railways are sold to adults. Manufacturers 80 from Europe and from countries as far afield as Japan 90 are finding a ready market for their model toys here. 100 The latest to catch on are radio controlled cars. It 110 seems that men, whatever their age, remain boys at heart 120 throughout their lives.   123 words

FACILITY DRILL 30a:

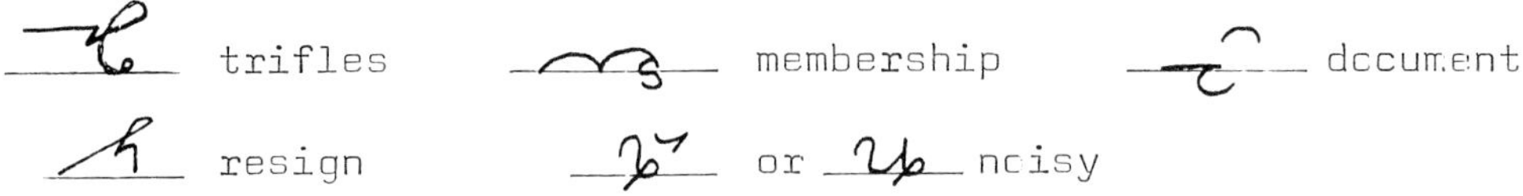

     trifles   membership   document

     resign   or   noisy

PASSAGE 30a: (to follow Page 71, textbook)

This season we sent out to all our members a 10 copy of the new regulations which were adopted at the 20 last committee meeting. It was a noisy session and there 30 was a lot of discussion and the wording of some 40 sections was adapted slightly before the Chairman finally signed the 50 document. No-one is likely to resign membership because of 60 the alterations, although it is amazing how easily some people 70 seem to take offence where none is intended. Life is 80 too short to get upset about trifles. The only sensible 90 course to take is to make light of misunderstandings and 100 try to be amused by them.

106 words

End of Section 1

SECTION 2 : Secretarial and Commercial Material

FACILITY DRILL 31:　　or　　scientifically
young man　proficient　qualified　lecturer
or　outstanding　inventive　by accident　abbreviated
or　consequently　or　systematically
preface　19th Century　handwriting　languages
popularity　unnecessary　or　unfortunately

NOTE:
You will probably have noticed that words ending in LY can often be shortened
safely by leaving out the L - see 'consequently', 'systematically' and
'scientifically' above.   In future, therefore, only this contracted form
will be given in Facility Drills, although it is quite correct to use the
fuller outline, if this is preferred.

PASSAGE 31:

Teeline was invented by James Hill, who had learned Pitman's shorthand as a
young man, and who had become a proficient writer of it.   By studying in
his own time after a day's work, he qualified as a teacher of commercial
subjects by the time he was twenty, and began teaching shorthand and
economics in evening classes.

In those days, jobs were hard to find and wages generally were low, so the
extra teaching brought in a little more money; but he loved the work and was
very popular with his students, many of whom achieved outstanding success.
There were some, however, who found shorthand very difficult and it was
partly in order to help them and partly because he had a naturally inventive
mind, that he began to experiment in ways of making shorthand easier to learn.
Out of many years of research into this and from his interest in language
generally, came the discovery of Teeline.

By then he had been employed as a full-time lecturer in several Colleges,
and one day, he discovered, quite by accident, that some of his students

could write in abbreviated longhand[190] almost as quickly as they could write shorthand.   Consequently, he[200] set about the task of systematically and scientifically applying work[210] study principles to ordinary longhand.   The results were amazing, and[220] in the preface to one of the early books he[230] wrote: "Teeline turns nineteenth century handwriting into a jet-age[240] tool, and could make the study of shorthand unnecessary."
Unfortunately,[250] he died before he had completed his work, but Teeline[260] has continued to grow in popularity and is taught in[270] many countries and in several languages.   Perhaps the day will[280] come when Teeline will be taught instead of ordinary writing[290] to children in school.   If so, then shorthand will indeed[300] have become unnecessary, because everyone will grow up knowing how[310] to write quickly and there will be no need to[320] study shorthand later in life.   325 words

HINT 6: As well as building your speed, you must also build stamina. You may find that you cannot manage the longer passages at the first attempt. Some-where along the way, you will tire, either physically or mentally, and fail to get the whole of the piece down.

In this case, try splitting it up into several sections. Work at each section until you can take it down at your target speed, following the pattern outline earlier.   Then try putting the whole piece together, section by section, until you can take the whole of it successfully.

FACILITY DRILL 32:

work study department	of the people	in the department
in all other departments	efficiently	manufactur
effective	equal/equally	or more	repetiti
continuously	or	similarly	or	typist
fans	tabulators	relevant	minim
loss of time	may be required	bonuses	housewi

PASSAGE 32:   Work Study

Many large factories have work study departments. The job of[10] the people employed in this department is to observe those[20] working in all other departments to see if the work[30] being done can be performed more efficiently.

If time can 40 be saved, then production can be improved, with a consequent 50 drop in the price of the goods being manufactured. In 60 these days of intense competition, the survival of a firm 70 can depend on such factors. But it is not only 80 in factories that work study is effective. It is equally 90 useful in the office and the efficient office worker will 100 be his or her own work study observer. For instance, 110 if envelopes are being addressed and the typist has to 120 turn each one over before placing it in the machine, 130 the seconds this takes may add up to perhaps ten 140 or more minutes on the whole job. This means that 150 ten minutes less is available for getting on with other 160 work.

So before starting on a repetitive task, work out 170 how time can be saved by placing the material close 180 at hand and arranging it so that one envelope or 190 form can be taken easily from the pile, enabling the 200 work to flow continuously.

Similarly, if one envelope is taken 210 out of the machine, before the next is fed in, 220 time is wasted. If the new envelope is inserted before 230 the previous one is completely removed, the work will be 240 speeded up and some of the typist's energy will be 250 saved.

If forms are being typed, bend the pile so 260 that it fans out, thus making it easy to lift 270 each sheet in turn. Feed in each form at the 280 same point and set tabulators so that the relevant sections 290 can be reached with the minimum loss of time. Thinking 300 on these lines also helps to make the work more 310 interesting. Saving time and energy becomes a challenge.

If a 320 job takes an hour, then apart from the cost of 330 the materials and postage, it also costs whatever that typist 340 is paid per hour. If a poor typist cannot get 350 through all the work, another typist may be required to 360 help. This means that two people have to be paid 370 for doing one job, so less money will be available 380 for wage increases or bonuses.

Even the housewife can ease 390 her work load by planning her day, so that she 400 has more time and energy left to use for herself. 410   <u>410 words</u>

FACILITY DRILL 33:

or conjures smart smarter

well-groomed or well-educated typewriter

applied responsibility or originally

PASSAGE 33: The Secretary

To most people, the word 'secretary' conjures up a picture /10 of a smart young woman, well-groomed and well-educated, /20 efficiently dealing with the various aspects of office work. This /30 may be a reasonable idea, though not all secretaries are /40 smart or young, and during the past thirty years or /50 so, the term has been applied very loosely to anyone, /60 however inefficient, whose work involved shorthand and typing.

At the /70 end of the last century, most secretaries were men, as /80 women were not usually employed in offices. It was the /90 invention of the typewriter which opened the door to women /100 entering the business world, and the ability to type well /110 and to take shorthand notes were the first and most /120 important qualifications required.

These early secretaries were expected to dress /130 very simply and in plain clothes, so as not to /140 distract their male colleagues. Today, a great deal more is /150 expected of a secretary. She must still be proficient in /160 office skills and work with, as well as for, her /170 boss; she must be tactful, able to speak correctly and /180 to spell, but she must be able also to handle /190 a continually increasing number of machines and to accept a /200 higher degree of responsibility. Not all colleges can provide training /210 in this, so the would-be secretary must be prepared /220 to go on learning after completing her college course and /230 keep herself up-to-date with new developments. As more /240 machines take over work which was originally done by people, /250 fewer secretaries will be required, so those who are employed /260 will have to be much smarter, better educated and more /270 highly efficient than ever before.   275 words

FACILITY DRILL 34:   large organisations   remark

within the company   confidential   apparently

PASSAGE 34: Secretaries

Secretaries come in various forms. In a large organisation, there /10 may be a secretarial pool, and each person in it /20 may act as secretary to several people within the company. /30 Those at the top of the organisation will have their /40 own secretaries who work only for them, and who may /50 have to handle a good many private and confidential matters. /60 It is important that these secretaries can be trusted not /70 to talk about company affairs outside the office. Not only /80 is it disloyal to pass on matters which are not /90 the concern of an outsider, but in these days of /100 intense business competition, a thoughtless remark or an apparently trivial /110 piece of information may be of great value to a /120 rival company. Spying goes on in the business world as /130 well as between nations, so it is as well to /140 be aware of the dangers of careless talk.

A company /150 secretary has a quite different role to play. This job /160 is almost always given to a man, who is responsible /170 for the general administration of the organisation which employs him. /180 He will check the company books and take minutes of /190 meetings and will have his own private secretary to deal /200 with correspondence and routine matters.

The Institute of Chartered Secretaries, /210 which was founded in the last century, runs its own /220 examinations. Those who pass and who have had the appropriate /230 amount of practical experience, are allowed to become Associates or /240 Fellows. The letters A.C.I.S. or F.C./250 I.S. after a person's name show that he has /260 fulfilled these requirements.

The London Chamber of Commerce runs Certificate /270 and Diploma examinations for personal and private secretaries. Possession of /280 these indicates to an employer that proper training has been /290 undertaken, and holders of these qualifications are entitled to become /300 members of the Institute of Qualified Private Secretaries. Anyone who /310 wishes to get to the top of the Secretarial profession /320 would be well advised to consider taking such an examination. /330

330 words

FACILITY DRILL 35:

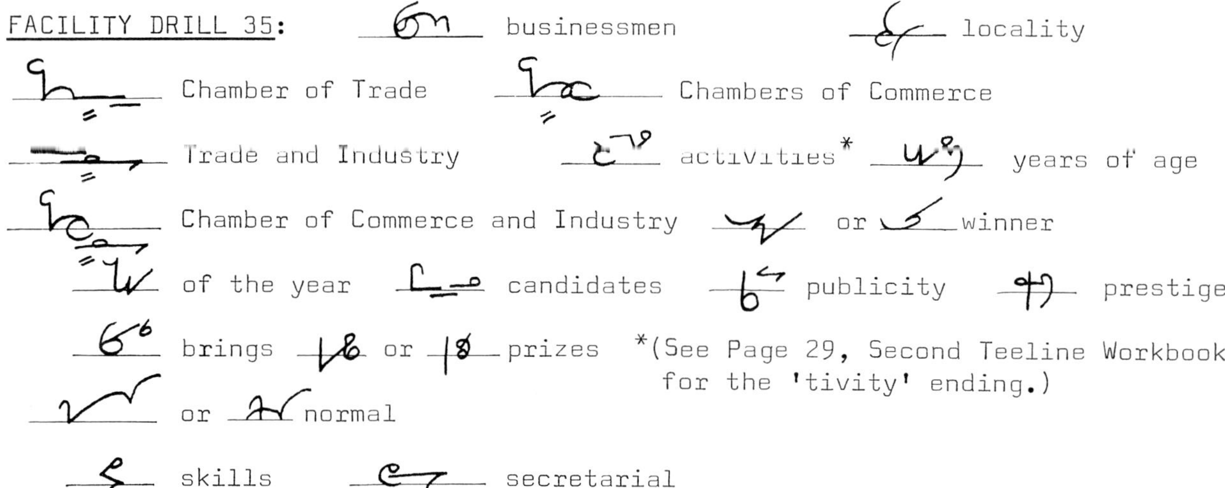

PASSAGE 35:   Chambers of Commerce

A Chamber of Commerce is an association of businessmen whose $\overset{10}{/}$ aim is to promote and protect trade interests in their $\overset{20}{/}$ own locality.   These organisa- tions may be members of the National $\overset{30}{/}$ Chamber of Trade, which was formed in 1897 $\overset{40}{/}$ to look after the interests of merchants and traders of $\overset{50}{/}$ all kinds. Many Chambers of Commerce have a Junior Section, $\overset{60}{/}$ which encourages young workers in trade and industry and those $\overset{70}{/}$ training for such work, to take an active part in $\overset{80}{/}$ the commercial activities of the locality.   Some hold competi- tions to $\overset{90}{/}$ find the secretary of the year.

One which was held $\overset{100}{/}$ recently set candidates the task of arranging an imaginar conference, $\overset{110}{/}$ for which they had several weeks to prepare the necessary $\overset{120}{/}$ programme and letters.   In addition, they were given a shorthand $\overset{130}{/}$ and type- writing test, a telephone test and an interview.

Winning $\overset{140}{/}$ such a competition brings publicity and prestige as well as $\overset{150}{/}$ many useful prizes.   The London Chamber of Commerce and Industry $\overset{160}{/}$ holds an annual competition to find the Top Secretary in $\overset{170}{/}$ Britain.   Hundreds of girls compe in this and one recent $\overset{180}{/}$ winner, though only 23 years of age, spoke three $\overset{190}{/}$ foreign languages, in addition to being proficient in the normal $\overset{200}{/}$ secretarial skills.

202 words

FACILITY DRILL 36:

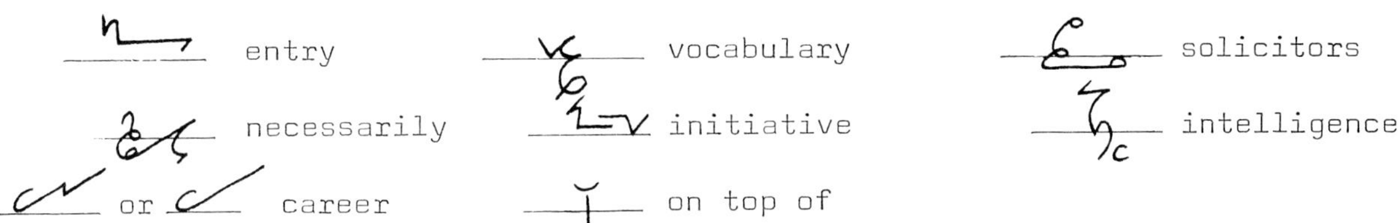

PASSAGE 36: Specialist Secretaries

Girls who want to be able to undertake really interesting [10] and well-paid jobs, should consider doing some specialist training [20] on top of their ordinary secretarial course.

Bi-lingual secretaries [30] can often obtain posts involving travel or working abroad. The [40] Teeline writer who already speaks a foreign language can easily [50] add foreign shorthand to her skills. Teeline adapts easily to [60] any language which uses the same alphabet as English and [70] there are several foreign language Teeline courses already available.

For [80] those with an interest in hospital work, a post as [90] medical secretary may be attractive. Many colleges run courses for [100] medical secretaries and entry to these is usually for those [110] with at least 80 w.p.m. shorthand speed and [120] a good knowledge of words, as the vocabulary required to [130] pass the medical secretarial examination is difficult. However, a good [140] medical secretary is never likely to be out of work. [150]

Others may prefer to work for a firm of solicitors [160] in which case they will need some training in legal [170] terms. Legal secretaries learn much about common law in the [180] course of their work and may find themselves acting in [190] minor matters on behalf of their boss, once they have [200] become experienced.

Office work does not necessarily mean taking down [210] and typing business letters all day. For the well qualified [220] woman with initiative and intelligence, many doors are open today [230] to an interesting, well-paid and worthwhile career.

238 words

FACILITY DRILL 37:

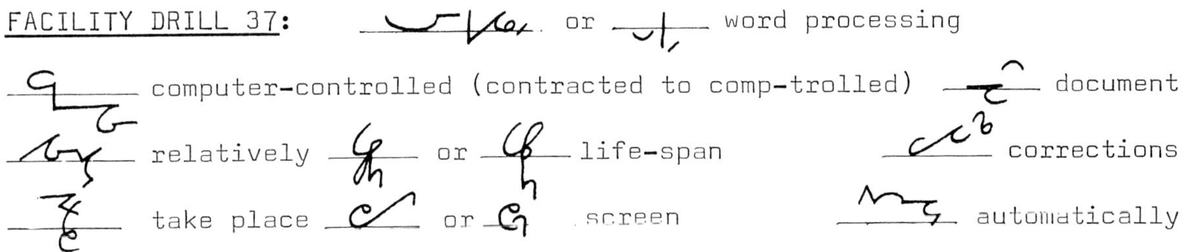

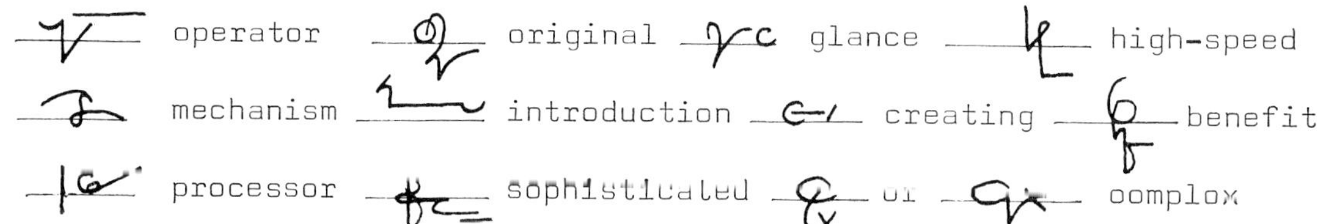

operator	original	glance	high-speed
mechanism	introduction	creating	benefit
processor	sophisticated	or	complex

PASSAGE 37: Word Processing Machines

Rising wages and the shortage of good secretaries are factors /[10] which have contributed to the development of word processing machines. /[20] These are computer-controlled typewriters which can work much faster /[30] and more efficiently than any secretary, but without getting tired /[40] or making mistakes. In their relatively short life-span, word /[50] processing machines have undergone many changes. The early systems were /[60] based on an ordinary typewriter, so that a document had /[70] to be played out on paper before any changes or /[80] corrections could take place. This meant that while a document /[90] was being printed out, the typewriter mechanism could not be /[100] used for any other purpose. Today's machines have a screen /[110] which allows the operator to see the original typed document /[120] at a glance. So, changes can be made in less /[130] time and the newly arranged document run off automatically on /[140] a separate high-speed printer. This allows the operator to /[150] go on processing new work at the same time as /[160] printing is taking place, whith the result that more work /[170] is done in less time than previously.

The introduction of /[180] word processing machines is creating a demand for skilled operators, /[190] who should have the ability to spell and carry out /[200] complex instructions, as well as being fast and accurate typists. /[210] The word processor is a sophisticated piece of equipment, which /[220] needs proper handling if it is to be of maximum /[230] benefit to its owners. <u>234 words</u>

<u>REMINDER</u>: Words not given in the Facility Drill will be found in the alphabetical word list in the textbook, TEELINE, and groupings in the alphabetical word grouping list at the back of SECOND TEELINE WORKBOOK.

FACILITY DRILL 38:

made their	appearance	installed	world-wide
rooms	computers	airports	up-to-the-minute

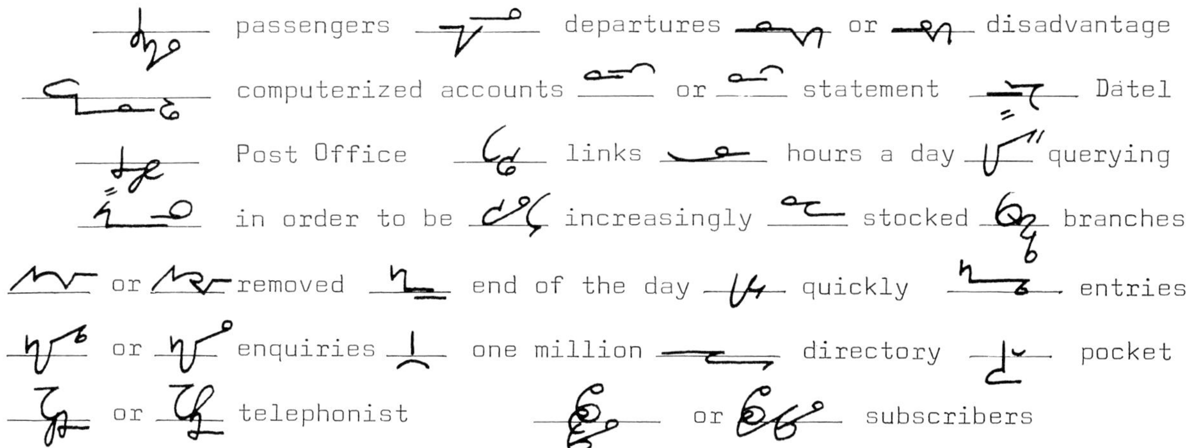

PASSAGE 38: Computers

It does not seem very long ago since computers made / their appearance. The early ones were very large and expensive / machines. I remember being taken to see one which had / just been installed in the offices of a world-wide / trading concern, and which would have filled any of the / rooms in my house. Today's computers are usually much smaller / and cheaper and their use is extending yearly.

They can / be seen at railway stations and airports, giving up-to/-the minute information to passengers on arrivals and departures. They / tell the airport staff who check in luggage, which seats / are still available on the plane.   Most banks have changed / to computerized accounts, which save storage space, but which have / the disadvantage that if a customer is querying a statement / the bank's own record of transactions has to be screened / in order to be read.

The Post Office provides a / useful Datel service which links computers by special telephone lines / across the whole of Britain and which operates for twenty/-four hours a day. This service is being used increasingly / by retailers to keep their shops well stocked. For instance, / a customer may buy an item of clothing bearing a / special tag, which is removed when the purchase is made./ At the end of the day, all these tags are / fed into a computer, which records what has been sold./ This allows the firm to know at any given moment / what needs replacing in each of its branches. The orders / for new stock can also be made by computer.

The²⁶⁰ latest use of computers by the Post Office is to²⁷⁰ store directory entries, to save the operator from having to²⁸⁰ search through books. As the number of enquiries is increasing²⁹⁰ by about one million a year, it is becoming impossible³⁰⁰ to have a complete set of telephone directories within the³¹⁰ reach of every telephonist on that particular job. If the³²⁰ experiment is successful, subscribers should find the information they require³³⁰ can be provided very much more quickly than at present,³⁴⁰ and the operator's work will be made easier.

The pocket³⁵⁰ computer is a development which the majority of us could³⁶⁰ not have foreseen twenty years ago. Who knows what further³⁷⁰ developments in this area the next twenty years will bring.³⁸⁰

__380 words__

FACILITY DRILL 39:

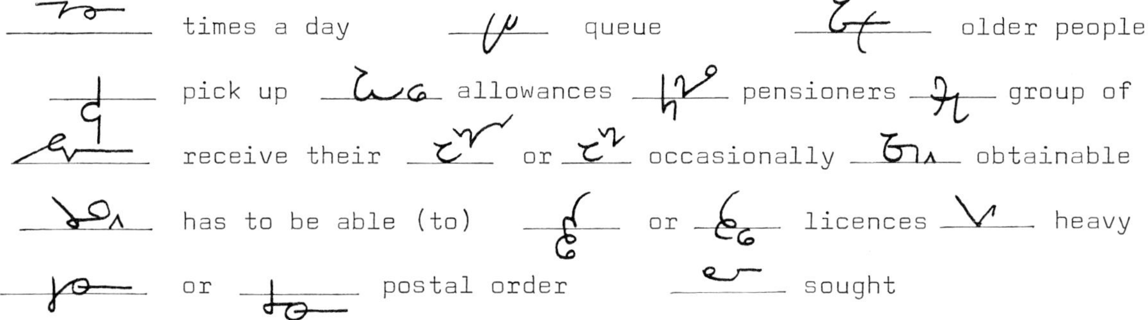

	times a day		queue		older people
	pick up		allowances		pensioners		group of
	receive their		or		occasionally		obtainable
	has to be able (to)		or		licences		heavy
	or		postal order		sought

PASSAGE 39: The Post Office

On most days in the week I go to my¹⁰ local Post Office, which is also a general store. Outside²⁰ is the post box, which is cleared several times a³⁰ day by a visiting postman in a van. Sometimes I⁴⁰ simply put my letters into the box and come home⁵⁰ again, but sometimes I have to go to the counter⁶⁰ to get a package weighed, or to buy stamps. How⁷⁰ long I have to wait depends on the day and⁸⁰ the time at which I arrive.

On Mondays, there is⁹⁰ usually a queue of older people waiting to pick up¹⁰⁰ their pensions. On Tuesdays, mothers collect their child benefits and¹¹⁰ on Thursdays another group of pensioners receive their payments.

Occasionally¹²⁰ I have to cash a postal order or pay a¹³⁰ cheque into my Post Office savings account. Now and then,¹⁴⁰ I buy some National Savings Certifica⌐ or draw some money¹⁵⁰ out of my savings account. The postmaster or postmistress has [160] to be able to deal with all these items, and, [170] in addition, must handle payment for television licences and telephone [180] bills. Even the water rate can be paid through the [190] Post Office.

Not all post offices handle all the documents [200] which are obtainable. For car or dog licences, for example, [210] it is often necessary to apply to one of the [220] larger branches, but the work load in any branch is [230] heavy and the staff require special training for the job. [240] Nevertheless, it is interesting work for those who enjoy contact [250] with people, for the local Post Office often becomes the [260] centre where help and advice are sought by the community [270] generally.

271 words

FACILITY DRILL 40:

over thirty million — over half a million
(the a is inserted to make clear
or delivered — more than   that this is not 6 million.)

over one hundred thousand — twenty-one million

circumstances — over ninety per cent — first-class

Fridays — liable — delivery — or — second-class

third day — two hundred thousand — telecommunications

calls a day — dialled — direct-dialling

in this department — Prestel — facts and figures

in the world — engineers — maintenance — Girobank

over-loaded — irritating — in view (of the)

nationalised — astray (the final a is better omitted in this
outline.)

Great Britain

PASSAGE 40:   The Work of the Post Office in Great Britain

Every working day, over thirty million letters and over half [10] a million parcels are handled by the Post Office in [20] Great Britain. These are collected from over one hundred thousand [30] post boxes and delivered to more than twenty-one million [40] addresses all over the country.

In normal circumstances, the aim is for over ninety per cent of first-class letters to be delivered the following day, although letters posted on Fridays are liable to be held up until the following Monday, because there is only one delivery on Saturdays. Second-class letters can take up to a week to reach their destinations, although the aim is to deliver them by the third day after they have been collected.

But the postal service is only one branch of the total work of the Post Office. The telecommunications service currently employs over two-hundred-thousand staff and handles over fifty million calls a day. Most calls can be dialled direct by the customer, and this direct-dialling service has been extended to include many overseas countries. A new service being planned in this department is one linking the telephone to television so that up-to-date facts and figures on a variety of topics can be brought into the home. It is to be known as PRESTEL, and will be the first public service of its kind in the world.

In order to maintain the telephone service, the Post Office employs some eighty thousand engineers and maintenance men.

The Girobank is the third main section of the Post Office, which has grown yearly since it was first introduced some ten years ago. It is through this bank that people without personal banking accounts can pay bills, which saves them having to buy postal or money orders or having to make a long journey to some office to pay in cash.

Small wonder then that sometimes mistakes occur, letters go astray, or telephone lines become over-crowded, preventing us from making the call we want to. Irritating though this is, perhaps at such times we should remind ourselves that the occasions on which we have to suffer such inconvenience are relatively rare, in view of the vast amount of business which is handled daily.

The figures given here are the latest available, but they are already out-of-date. As the years go by, it is likely that there will be a significant growth not only in these sections, but in the number of new ventures to be undertaken by this nationalised industry.

420 words

FACILITY DRILL 41:

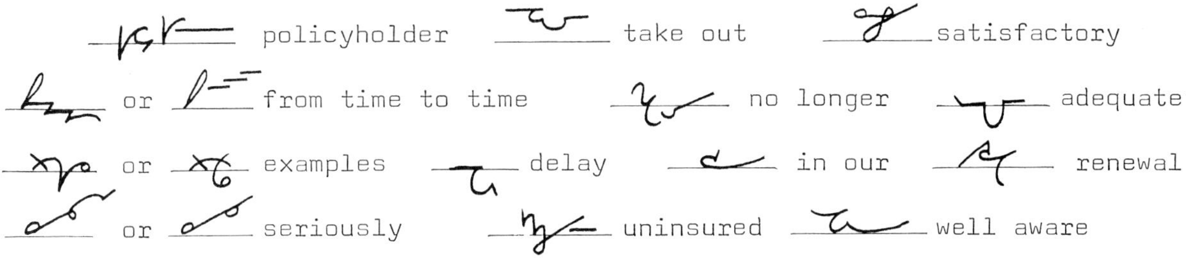

PASSAGE 41: Insurance Letter (1)

Dear Policyholder,

We are sure that you are well aware ^{10} of the constant rise in prices, but have you considered ^{20} how these rises affect your insurance cover?

Many people take ^{30} out a policy on their home and its contents, but ^{40} fail to realise that if this is to give satisfactory ^{50} cover, it has to be adjusted from time to time. ^{60} The sums for which homes were insured even five years ^{70} ago are no longer adequate.

We enclose with this letter ^{80} a booklet giving clear instructions for estimating the present cost ^{90} of rebuilding, should your home be destroyed by fire and ^{100} also how to assess the value of the contents of ^{110} your home. If you follow the examples given in our ^{120} tables, you can work out for yourself whether the present ^{130} amount quoted on your policy is sufficient.

If not, then ^{140} we urge you, in your own interests, to inform us ^{150} on the attached slip, what you would like it to ^{160} be. There will be no extra premium to pay until ^{170} your next policy renewal date. Act now. Delay could cause ^{180} you to find yourself seriously uninsured, should any misfortune involving ^{190} your home occur.

Yours sincerely,   <u>195 words</u>

Learning Hint:

Wherever possible, note your transcription time and work out what your transcription speed is in words a minute. For instance, if it takes you ten minutes to write back 240 words, it will be 240 divided by 10, i.e. 24 w.p.m.

If you are preparing for a speed examination, note how many words you will have to transcribe in the examination and how long you will be allowed for the transcription. Divide the number of words by the time allowed and see if your own transcription rate is enough to enable you to complete the examination in the time allowed. If not, you will have to speed up your transcription rate.

The best way to do this is to write clear outlines, so that you do not waste time in trying to decipher your Teeline notes.

FACILITY DRILL 42:

ever-increasing   replacing   or   leaflet

or   burgled   index-linked   participate

or   Government's   or   inflation   or   confirming

information   free of charge   or   informed

or   present-time   protection   advantage

PASSAGE 42: Insurance Letter (2)

Dear Policyholder,

We enclose with this letter a leaflet which /explains how you can protect yourself against the ever-increasing /costs of replacing household goods if your house was to /be burgled or suffer some serious damage.

There is little /doubt that prices are going to continue to rise, so /we have worked out a scheme by which, for no /extra charge, your policy can b index-linked to changes /in costs. Our figures will be drawn each month from /the Government's Retail Prices Index. If you decide to participate /i this plan, we can adjust the amount of cover /to keep it in line with inflati This will save /you from having to make the necessary adjustments yourself each /year.

All you need to do is to return the / enclosed card to us, confirming that the particulars on it / are correct at the present time. Once you have paid / your premium for the coming year, you can then forget / about it until the nex renewal date, when you will / be informed what the next premium will be. In the / meantime, cover will be adjusted monthly, free of charge. You / will see, if you study the information given on the / enclosed leaflet, how easily and quickly the sum insured can / become out of date. Ind linking will protect you from / falling into this trap. We hope you will take advantage / of the protection it offers. We look forward to hearing / from yc

Yours sincerely,   <u>244 words</u>

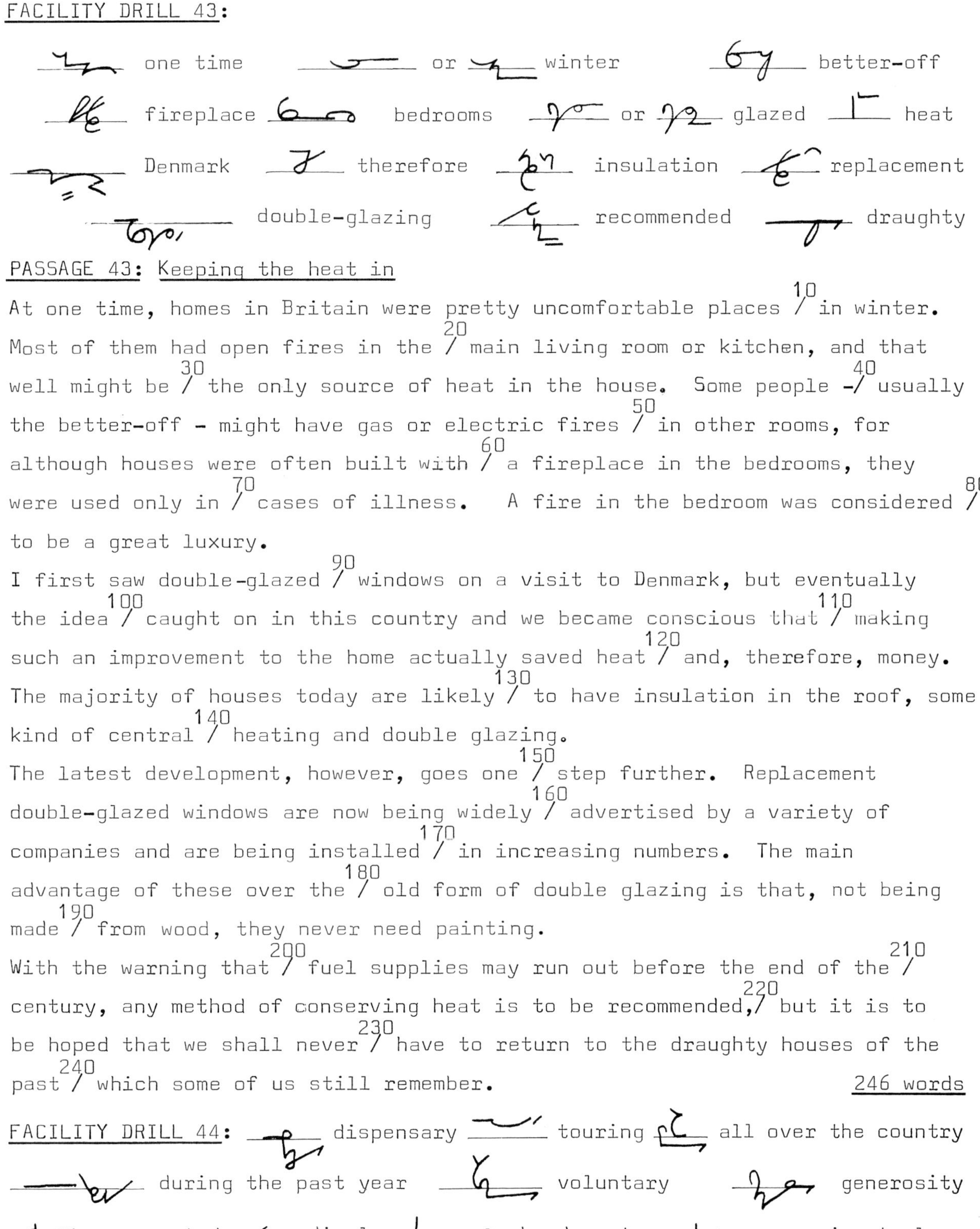

FACILITY DRILL 43:

one time ___ or ___ winter ___ better-off

fireplace ___ bedrooms ___ or ___ glazed ___ heat

___ Denmark ___ therefore ___ insulation ___ replacement

___ double-glazing ___ recommended ___ draughty

PASSAGE 43: Keeping the heat in

At one time, homes in Britain were pretty uncomfortable places / in winter.
Most of them had open fires in the / main living room or kitchen, and that
well might be / the only source of heat in the house. Some people -/ usually
the better-off - might have gas or electric fires / in other rooms, for
although houses were often built with / a fireplace in the bedrooms, they
were used only in / cases of illness.   A fire in the bedroom was considered /
to be a great luxury.

I first saw double-glazed / windows on a visit to Denmark, but eventually
the idea / caught on in this country and we became conscious that / making
such an improvement to the home actually saved heat / and, therefore, money.

The majority of houses today are likely / to have insulation in the roof, some
kind of central / heating and double glazing.

The latest development, however, goes one / step further. Replacement
double-glazed windows are now being widely / advertised by a variety of
companies and are being installed / in increasing numbers. The main
advantage of these over the / old form of double glazing is that, not being
made / from wood, they never need painting.

With the warning that / fuel supplies may run out before the end of the /
century, any method of conserving heat is to be recommended, / but it is to
be hoped that we shall never / have to return to the draughty houses of the
past / which some of us still remember.   **246 words**

FACILITY DRILL 44: ___ dispensary ___ touring ___ all over the country

___ during the past year ___ voluntary ___ generosity

___ unwanted ___ display ___ headquarters ___ prominent place

PASSAGE 44:   Letter about the P.D.S.A.

Dear Sir or Madam,

   You are, no doubt, familiar with / our charity, the People's Dispensary for Sick Animals. Our vans / have been touring your district for many years, collecting your / jumble, which helps to maintain over 60 treatment centres and / homes for stray animals all over the country.

   During the / past year, nearly a million sick animals have been treated / by the P.D.S.A.   In the majority of / cases, their owners have been too poor to afford the / services of a private 'vet' and it is a fact / that, but for the generosity of the general public, in / supporting us, many of their pets would have died.

   We / rely on voluntary contributions of unwanted articles, but we also / welcome donations. Our van will be in your area next / Tuesday. If you have anything for us to collect, please / display this leaflet in a prominent place and if you / would care to make a donation to our work, send / it, with your name and address to our headquarters at / the address given on the enclosed form. However small your / contribution, it will be gratefully received.

                              Yours sincerely,   188 words

FACILITY DRILL 45:

lengthy   agenda   legally   verbatim

resolutions   or   amendments   relevant

PASSAGE 45: The taking and recording of Minutes

Minutes are a record of decisions reached at formal meetings, 10 and it is the duty of the person chosen to 20 act as secretary to make notes as the meeting proceeds, 30 so that after the meeting, accurate Minutes can be prepared. 40 It used to be the custom for Minutes to be 50 written up in a special book reserved for this purpose, 60 but it is more usual nowadays, for them to be 70 typed and copies are often circulated to all committee members 80 before they attend the next meeting.

Minutes need not be 90 lengthy reports of everything which was said and by whom. 100 All that is essential is that they should clearly state 110 the date a place of the meeting, the number or 120 names of those present, the matters

discussed and the decisions[130] reached. They should follow the order of the agenda for[140] that meeting and should be accurate and clearly understood, since[150] once they have been accepted by the members and signed[160] by the Chairman, they are legally binding.
It is not[170] usually necessary for the secretary to be a shorthand writer[180] as verbatim notes may be required only to record the[190] actual wording of resolutions put to the meeting and any[200] amendments made, since these will be relevant to the decisions[210] reached. It is a definite advantage, however, to be able[220] to take a shorthand note, when required.
It is a[230] good plan for the secretary to prepare the Minutes as[240] soon as possible after the meeting while events are still[250] fresh in her memory, and to use the agenda as[260] a guide.   262 words

<u>FACILITY DRILL 46</u>:

to the fact (that)   proud   founder members

early days   successive committees   decade

leadership   membership   recruiting drive

critical   bothered   folk   coming year

<u>PASSAGE 46</u>:   <u>Speech about falling membership</u>
Ladies and Gentlemen, it is now five years since our[10] Association came into being.   We must face up to the[20] fact that we have not made the progress we all[30] hoped for during those five years. We would be deluding[40] ourselves if we thought an increase in membership of twenty[50] people in half a decade was something to be proud[60] of. Those of us who were founder members will recall[70] the great enthusiasm of those early days and the feelings[80] of confidence in the future of the Association. What went[90] wrong? I cannot agree with those people who say that[100] successive committees have failed to provide the kind of leadership[110] we need.   I believe the fault lies with the ordinary[120] members who have failed to give the committee the backing[130] it deserves.   Take our Annual General Meeting as an example.[140] Out of a total membership of one hundred and sixty,[150] a mere thirty-four people bothered to attend, and no[160] fewer than ten of those thirty-four people were members[170] of

the committee. I think we have reached a critical[180] point in the existence
of our Association, ladies and gentlemen.[190]
A successful recruiting drive during the coming year is, as[200] far as I can
see, the only thing which can[210] save the Association. We need young folk with
new ideas[220] and lots of enthusiasm. I shall be interested to hear[230] what
other members think about having a big recruiting drive.[240]   240 words

FACILITY DRILL 47:

______ successful   ______ lines of communication   ______ established

______ Chairman of the Board   ______ function

PASSAGE 47:   Lines of Communication

To be successful, every business must have efficient lines of[10] communication.
From the Chairman of the Board to the most[20] junior member of the staff, there
should be a path,[30] however indirect, which can serve as a channel for
instructions,[40] suggestions and reports. Even when such a channel for
communication[50] does exist, it is too often concerned with one-way[60] traffic
only. That is to say, it allows commands which[70] are issued at the top level
to travel down to[80] the lower levels, but it does not allow for the[90] reaction
to those commands to be sent back to the[100] level from which they came. If
there is a lack[110] of contact between the different levels of a business, then[120]
it is unlikely that the business will be a successful[130] one. Every member of
the staff should be able to[140] do something to ensure that lines of communication
are established[150] within a firm and that they function with maximum efficiency.[160]
                                                            160 words

FACILITY DRILL 48:

______ we are now   ______ Senior Planner   ______ County Council

______ applicant   ______ life assurance   ______ statistical

______ or ______ candidate   ______ or ______ officer   ______ minimum

PASSAGE 48:   Notice about Vacancy

We are now accepting applications for the post of Senior[10] Planner in the
County Council Planning Department. The successful applicant[20] will be

responsible to the Chief Planning Officer and will /30 be especially concerned with long-term population and housing forecasts./40 We are seeking a suitably qualified person with considerable experience /50 in this field, who is capable of working with the /60 minimum of supervision. Adequate assistance with the preparation of statistical /70 information will be provided and the appointed candidate will find /80 plenty of scope to develop his own ideas and to /90 participate in relevant research.   A generous grant will be given /100 towards the cost of removal expenses, and rented housing will /110 be available. Life assurance and superannuation schemes are in operation./120   120 words

<u>FACILITY DRILL 49:</u>

_____ recently been   _____ of the Society _____ or _____ criticism

_____ of the committee   _____ your committee   _____ to the Society

_____ critics   _____ democratically

<u>PASSAGE 49:</u>   <u>Speech in committee</u>

Madam Chairman, Ladies and Gentlemen, This committee has recently been /10 attacked over the way it has conducted the affairs of /20 the Society. Now I know that the next speaker will /30 have something to say about this, but perhaps you would /40 spare one or two moments to listen to what I /50 have to say about the matter.
As one of the /60 longest-standing members of the committee, I feel that I /70 am in a good position to tell whether or not /80 the kind of criticism which has been levelled at us /90 is justified.   Ladies and gentlemen, in the past, your committee /100 has done a lot of work which has been of /110 great benefit to the Society. Some of the things we /120 have done have been of a controversial nature, and I /130 would be the last person to try to deny that /140 fact. However, we have always listened carefully to what our /150 critics had to say, even if we did not always /160 take their advice. After all, we must remember that committee /170 members are democratically elected, and they are elected to govern./180   180 words

<u>FACILITY DRILL 50:</u> _____ tendency _____ or _____ confirmed _____ oral

_____ or _____ taxi _____ incoming _____ misunderstand _____ mishear

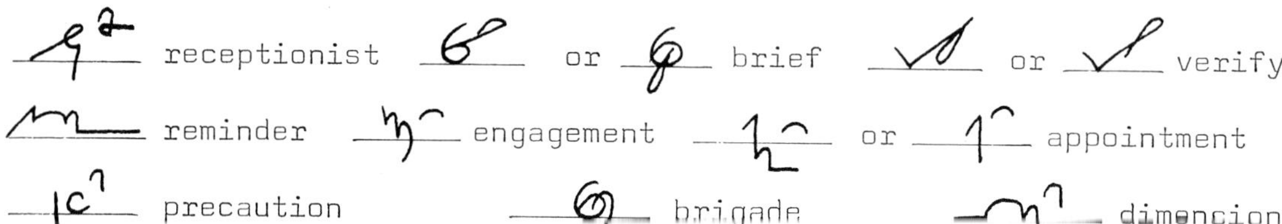

PASSAGE 50: Make a note of it.

There used to be a popular saying - 'Never put off /till tomorrow what you can do today', which was changed /by some wit to 'Never put off till tomorrow what /you can do the day after'. There are some firms /who seem to have adopted the latter saying as their /motto, for it seems to take them weeks, rather than /days, to reply to any letters sent to them, or /to deal with any orders placed with them. There is /also the tendency today for people to use the telephone /rather than bother to write a letter, and while there /are advantages in this, any decision taken by telephone, or /in a meeting, should be recorded or confirmed in writing /as soon as possible afterwards. A telephone conversation or an /oral discussion carries little or no weight in law. Anything /which is of any importance should be in writing. It /is also very easy to misunderstand or to mishear what /has been said, and putting it into a written form /not only clears up any mistakes, but helps to clarify /the discussion in the mind of the writer. Sometimes the /act of writing things down raises a query or reveals /a problem which had been over-looked during the conversation.

In /business, where numerous telephone discussions, possibly of a similar nature, /take place in a day, each one needs to be /noted immediately, or there is a danger that something will /be forgotten, or orders mixed up. Imagine what might happen /for instance, if the receptionist working for a taxi firm /did not make a note of each caller's requirements at /the time the call was received. Similarly, an efficient secretary /will keep a pad by the telephone on which to /note each incoming and outgoing call, the time it was /made and a brief summary of its purpose. This is /frequently useful if one needs to verify just when an /order was placed or a discussion took place. It is /helpful too, from time to time, to take stock of /what needs to be done in the coming week or /month and to make a reminder note, possibly in the /desk diary or on a calendar. Most business people keep /engagement

books, but it is easy to overlook an appointment [380] if it has been made a
long time ahead, and [390] checking up week by week is not only a wise [400]
precaution but shows how much time will be left for [410] other work when
appointments and routine matters have been dealt [420] with.
If you are one of the 'putting off till [430] tomorrow' brigade, why not turn
over a new leaf and [440] start to organise your life a little?   You will be [450]
surprised how much time you save by spending just a [460] little on planning
what is to come and recording what [470] has just gone; and getting some order
into your everyday [480] life should make you a great deal more valuable to [490]
your employer.   Why overload your memory and risk forgetting something [500]
important? Make a note of it and add a new [510] dimension to your life.

<u>514 words</u>

<u>FACILITY DRILL 51:</u>

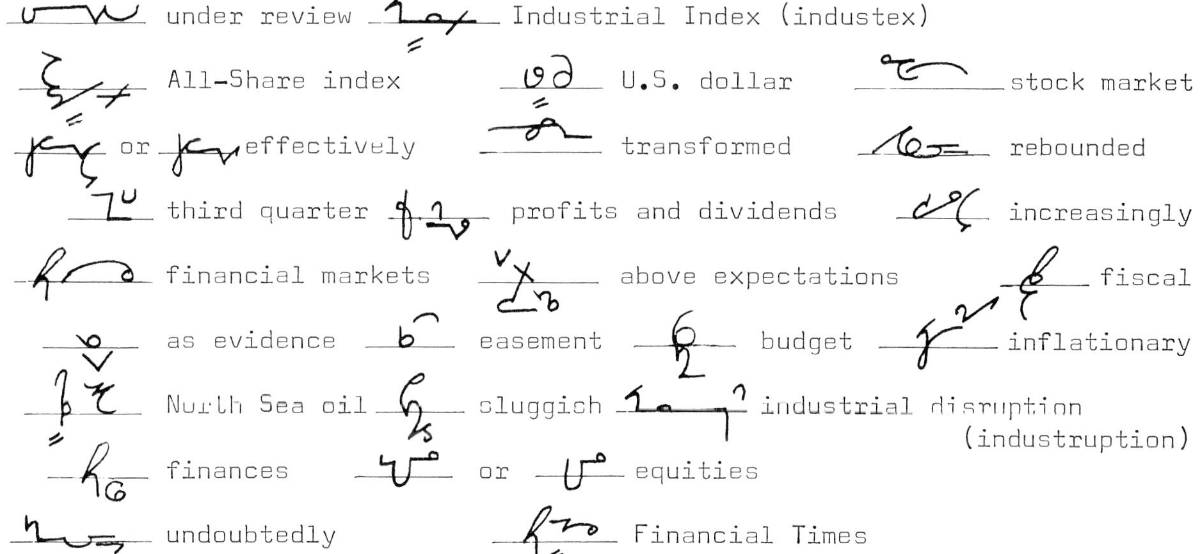

under review — Industrial Index (industex)
All-Share index — U.S. dollar — stock market
or effectively — transformed — rebounded
third quarter — profits and dividends — increasingly
financial markets — above expectations — fiscal
as evidence — easement — budget — inflationary
North Sea oil — sluggish — industrial disruption
(industruption)
finances — or — equities
undoubtedly — Financial Times

<u>PASSAGE 51:</u> <u>Extract from Manager's Report (1)</u>

The composition of the Trust Fund at 14th January, 19/80, is set out in [10]
Section 2 of this Report / and is followed by details of the changes in the / [30]
Trust's investments during the half-year. [20]
During the six months / under review, the Dow Jones Industrial Index rose by [40]
1/.7% while in London the Financial Times / All-Share Index fell by 4.1%./ [50] [60] [70]
The price of the units fell 2.5%./   Currency changes were again a major [80]

influence. Sterling was strong 90/ against the U.S. dollar and the dollar premium, which 100/ began the period at 9¾%, 110/ was finally abolished for over-seas investments in October. As a 120/ result, for the U.K. investor, the rise in the 130/ U.S. stock market over the period would have been 140/ effectively transformed into a decline of some 5% 150/ in the value of his holdings.

In the United States 160/ economic growth rebounded sharply during the third quarter of 19 170/79 and as company profits and dividends came in above 180/ expectations the stock market was firm.

In the United Kingdom, 190/ financial markets became increasingly unsettled during the summer, as evidence 200/ mounted that the proposed cutbacks in public expenditure were not 210/ being achieved and that therefore, monetary policy control was too 220/ relaxed, in view of the fiscal easement given in the 230/ June budget. At the same time, strongly rising energy costs 240/ and a continued high level of wage settlements were again 250/ leading to rising inflationary pressures despite the strength in sterling 260/ and the benefits of North Sea oil. As a result, 270/ there was a sharp increase in Bank Minimum Lending Rate 280/ to 17% which caused markets to weaken further. 290/ Combined with sluggish economic growth and increasing industrial disruption, company 300/ profits and finances were placed under severe strain. Share prices 310/ would undoubtedly have fallen further if dividends had not been 320/ raised sharply on the removal of controls in August, which 330/ placed equities on a more favourable return basis in relation 340/ to other financial assets.

344 words

FACILITY DRILL 52:   industrial ordinary index (indust/ord/ex)

payable   emphasised   into consideration

of the companies   erratic dividend   reinvestment

that the amount   year to year (Note: year after year)

interest rates   predictably   sensitive

or focused   equity markets   haven

ordinary index   institutional   portfolio

_______ irreparably   _______ correspondingly   _______ abatement

_______ recessionary   _______ unwelcome   _______ rewards   _______ uncertain

<u>PASSAGE 52:</u> <u>Extract from Manager's Report (2)</u>

This report covers the period from 18th June to 28th /(10) December, 1979,
during which the offered price of /(20) the Income units fell from 115/.1 pence /(30)
to 111.7 /(40) pence, a fall of 3.0 per cent. Over /(50) the same period the
Financial Times Industrial Ordinary Index /(60) fell by 13.3 per cent, whilst
the F.T. /(70) All-Share Index fell by 7.5 per cent./(80)

The interim distribution on income units for the year which /(90) ends on 15th
June, 1980, is 1.5 /(100) pence net per unit, payable on 20th February, 1980./(110)
Last year the interim payment was 1.0 pence./(120)

It should be possible at least to maintain last year's /(130) final payment of
1.75 pence net to /(140) give a total distribution of 3.25 pence /(150) for the year,
compared with 2.75 pence /(160) for the previous year. However, it must be
emphasised that /(170) when investments are selected for Recovery Fund we do not /(180)
take income into consideration. Many of the companies whose shares /(190) are
held have erratic dividend records, so that the amount /(200) of income available
for distribution or reinvestment may vary considerably /(210) from year to year.
Unit trusts are not permitted to /(220) build up reserves in order to eliminate
fluctuations in payments /(230) to unit-holders.

Rather as we suspected, last year closed /(240) on a gloomy note with domestic
interest rates at an /(250) all-time high and industrial disruption accompanying
efforts to restrain inflation./(260) Less predictably, unrest in sensitive areas
of the world focused /(270) investment attention on commodities, and particularly
gold, the traditional haven /(280) for funds in times of international disquiet.
Against this background, /(290) it was hardly surprising that the U.K. equity
market, /(300) as measured by the F.T. Ordinary Index, fell by /(310) about 13% in the
second half of the /(320) year.   Indeed, having regard to such a depressing
outlook, had /(330) it not been for the considerable level of institutional
liquidity, /(340) constantly fuelled by inflation, one could well have expected
a /(350) much weaker equity market. However, lessons drawn from the sharp /(360)
fall in markets during previous years illustrate that a carefully /(370) selected

portfolio of equities can immunize investors against the worst ^{380}/ effects of inflation. Equity investment, after all, represents a share ^{390}/ in assets that are usually impossible to replace except at ^{400}/ inflated values; provided the earning capacity of these assets is ^{410}/ not irreparably damaged by inflation their value should correspondingly increase. ^{420}/
It is difficult to foresee much abatement in the rate ^{430}/ of inflation during the coming year, although recessionary forces are ^{440}/ gaining in strength. Generally this will be unwelcome for the ^{450}/ weaker companies that, by definition, constitute the portfolio of Recovery ^{460}/ Fund and it is likely that a greater than usual ^{470}/ degree of liquidity will be held in order to take ^{480}/ advantage of new recovery opportunities that will surely occur.
It ^{490}/ is in such uncertain times that the spread of risk ^{500}/ afforded by a unit trust becomes valuable to investors who ^{510}/ wish to accept a higher than usual degree of risk ^{520}/ in search of better than average rewards.   <u>527 words</u>

<u>FACILITY DRILL 53</u>: _______ financial position

_______ the Chairman said _______ employees _______ Publicity Department

_______ or _______ optimistic _______ recommend a dividend _______ volume of trade

_______ home market _______ overseas sales _______ to bring about

_______ one million dollars _______ objectives _______ consolidate

_______ considerable amount _______ Board of Directors _______ of the Company

<u>PASSAGE 53</u>: <u>Chairman's Report</u>

The Chairman said: In presenting the very good trading figures ^{10}/ for last year, I wish to thank all employees of ^{20}/ the Company for the way they have worked to bring ^{30}/ about such a welcome improvement in our financial position.
In ^{40}/ particular, I wish to commend the work of the Publicity ^{50}/ Department which has done so much to bring our products ^{60}/ to the notice of a much wider section of the ^{70}/ general public. The Directors are pleased to recommend a dividend ^{80}/ of fifteen per cent, which is an increase of six ^{90}/ per cent over that of the previous year.
I am ^{100}/ very optimistic about our prospects during the current year. The ^{110}/

volume of trade in the home market should remain at [120] its present high level and we expect new opportunities to [130] occur in the field of exports. Your Board of Directors [140] has, therefore, set itself two main tasks for the coming [150] year: to consolidate our position at home and to increase [160] our overseas sales by making our products as well known [170] abroad as they are in this country.   I am confident [180] that the sum of one million dollars which we have [190] set aside for advertising will enable us to achieve both [200] objectives and to increase our turnover by a considerable amount. [210] <u>210 words</u>

FACILITY DRILL 54:

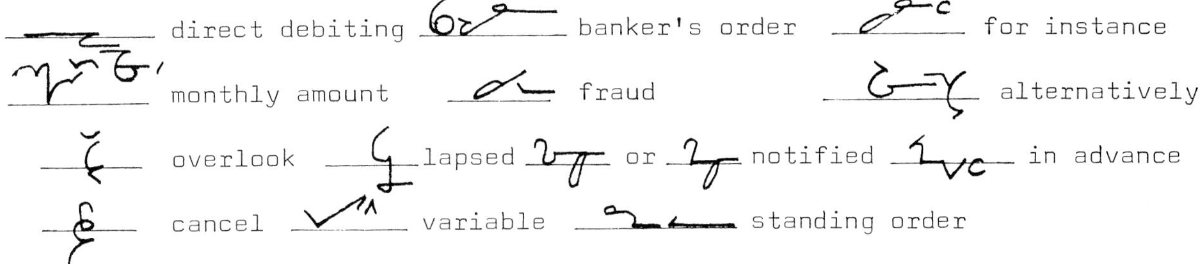

direct debiting   banker's order   for instance

monthly amount   fraud   alternatively

overlook   lapsed   or   notified   in advance

cancel   variable   standing order

PASSAGE 54: <u>Direct Debiting</u>

Most people who have banking accounts know about banker's orders, [10] whereby regular payments can be made on their behalf by [20] the bank.   For instance, if a customer pays a monthly [30] amount for the hire of a television set, having a [40] standing order at the bank saves him from having to [50] remember to write a cheque each month or, alternatively, to [60] remember to take his payment to the firm concerned. Once-[70]a-year payments, such as subscriptions to societies, are safer [80] dealt with in this way, as it is easy to [90] overlook them and to find oneself out of benefit or [100] a lapsed member.

These standing orders have worked very well [110] in the past, because most payments remained the same for [120] several years at a time, but one of the results [130] of the increased rate of inflation is that they now [140] tend to go up frequently.   This means that the customer [150] has to keep changing his instructions to the bank by [160] completing a new standing order form.

In order to avoid [170] this, a new system of direct debiting has been introduced, [180] so that, if the customer wishes, the bank can be [190] given the authority to pay whatever amount the organisation or [200] firm requests. The customer, however, must be notified in advance, [210] what the new payment will be, so that he can [220]

cancel his instructions to the bank if he is not [230] prepared to pay the
increased amount.
There are two methods [240] of direct debiting. One provides for the payment of
fixed [250] amounts, and the other for the payment of variable amounts. [260]
Paying bills in this way is simpler than paying them [270] by cheque or in cash;
it saves the customer the [280] trouble of constantly up-dating standing orders
and it has [290] been designed by the Banks to protect the customer against [300]
possible fraud.   <u>302 words</u>

FACILITY DRILL 55:

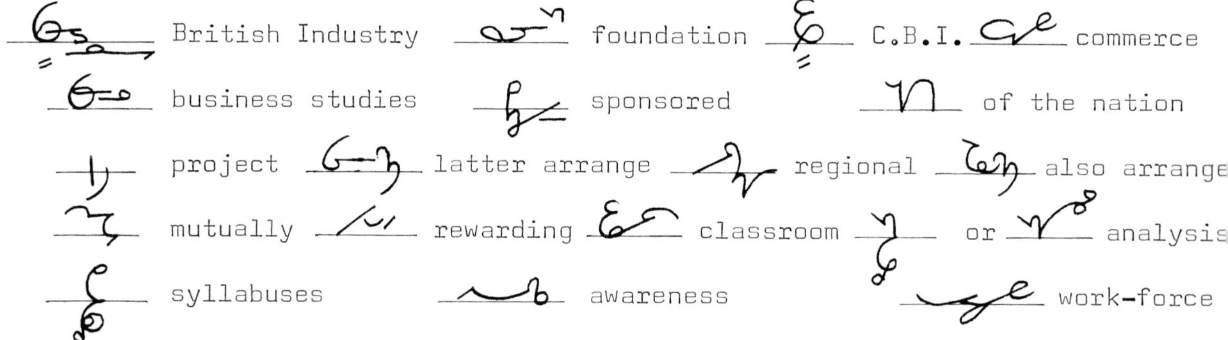

PASSAGE 55: <u>Understanding British Industry</u>

A new educational foundation sponsored by the C.B.I. [10] has been set up to help
teachers of commerce and [20] business studies to acquire a better understanding
of British industry [30] and the part it plays in the economic and social [40] life
of the nation.   The money for this project has [50] been subscribed by industrial
and commercial companies and has been [60] used for the provision of a main Centre
which supplies [70] books, films and other information to teachers for use in [80]
their schools and colleges, as well as for the setting- [90] up of regional centres.
The latter arrange for teachers to [100] be released from teaching to work in
factories and offices [110] so that they can experience at first-hand the kind [120] of
life many of their pupils will need to be [130] prepared for. They also arrange
for representatives from firms to [140] visit schools and colleges to see the kind
of work [150] which is being done there and, possibly, to give talks. [160]
Experiments on these lines have proved to be mutually rewarding. [170] The teachers
involved are now working on the provision of [180] suitable material for use in the
classroom, and an analysis [190] of examination syllabuses is being made to find out

if [200] the topics being covered and the questions being set are [210] relevant. Anything which increases a student's awareness of how industry [220] works and how it affects life generally, is to be [230] welcomed, for it should result in a future work-force [240] with a better understanding of the problems involved and may, [250] therefore, increase the chances of real co-operation between management and [260] employees.

<u>261 words</u>

<u>HINT 5</u>:

As soon as you hear a new word dictated, think of the letters you need. Once you have done this, write them as smoothly and quickly as you can, keeping a good controlled outline. Outlines which cannot be read back are useless. The more you use your Teeline, the more easily will outlines spring to mind when you hear the words, without the need to build them up first.   ALWAYS try to build up your own outline for a word, rather than look up the one given in a reference list.   Check, later, if you wish, to see that your outline is not more complicated than it need be, but remember that so long as you can get the dictation down correctly and read it back quickly and accurately, then YOUR outline must be right for you, and it does not matter if it is not the same as the one someone else prefers.

<u>End of Section 2</u>

SECTION 3 : General and Journalistic Material

<u>INTRODUCTORY DICTATION PASSAGE</u>:

<u>FACILITY DRILL</u>:

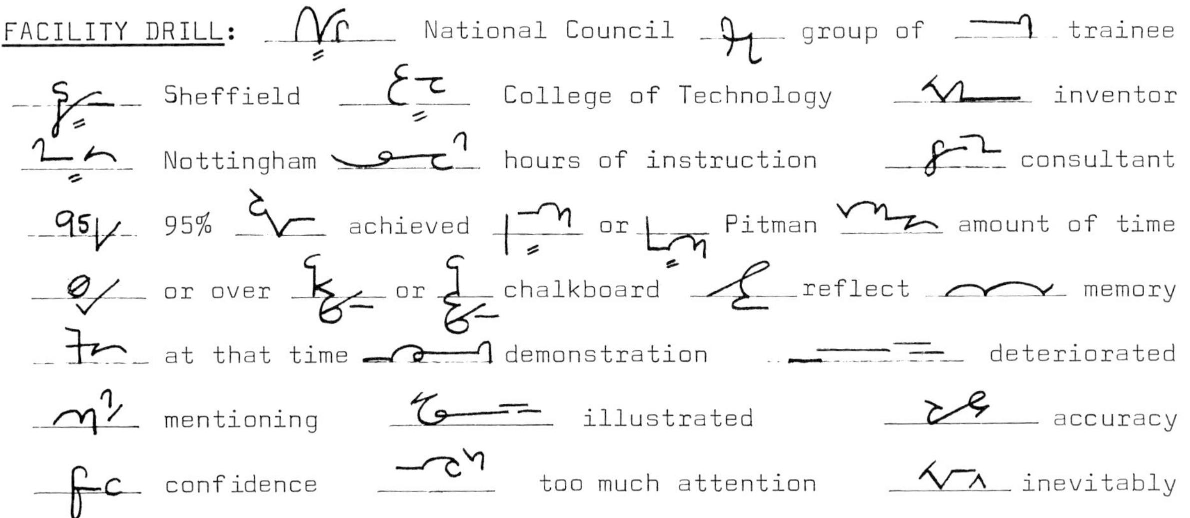

The first body to accept Teeline officially was the National /10 Council for the Training of Journalists. This happened in November /20 1968, after an experimen in teaching the system /30 to a group of trainee journalists who were taking a /4 block-release course at Sheffield College of Technology. These young /50 men knew no shorthand when they began their training in /60 September, and because they were being taught by the inventor /70 of Teeline himself, who had to travel from Nottingham to /80 give the lessons, they had instruction on only three days a week, for two hours each time.

At the end /100 of the eight-week course, and after only forty-two /110 hours of instruction, they were all tested on five-minute /120 passages by the National Council's own shorthand consultant. Two managed /130 the 70 w.a.m. passage and the rest transcribed /140 the 60 w.a.m. piece. None of them gained /150 less than 95% accuracy in transcription, one /160 achieved 100% and four 99% /170 or over. In the report sent to the National Council /180 the results were described as 'verging on the incredible', and /190 it was pointed out that Pitman writers woul not have /200 been able to complete their theory learning in the same /210 amount of time.

One must also remember that these students 220/ had no textbooks, because at that time, none had been 230/ published. They learned the principles from chalkboard demonstration and then 240/ worked from dictated words, sentences and passages, all of which 250/ they read back. Outlines which presented difficulty were then discussed 260/ and illustrated on the board.

In a follow-up investigation 270/ carried out some months later, newspaper personnel reported favourably on 280/ all these trainees, mentioning their ability to take direct 'quotes', 290/ their confidence in using the system and their enthusiasm for 300/ it.

It is sad to reflect that as the system 310/ has developed, accuracy in transcribing has tended to deteriorate in 320/ some areas. This may be because teaching does not always 330/ follow the lines laid down by the inventor. It is 340/ worth remembering that, using only the early simple form of 350/ Teeline, speeds of 100 w.a.m. and upwards 360/ were reached on four and five-minute passages, even by 370/ reporters for whom English was a foreign language. Too much 380/ attention to speed dodges too early is not to be 390/ recommended. The system, as laid down in the textbook, should 400/ be thoroughly mastered and the passages contained in it thoroughly 410/ drilled. This forms a wide vocabulary base on which speed 420/ can then be built, and only then should time be 430/ spent on learning the contracting devices, which, inevitably, increase the 440/ memory load. As James Hill once said - 'If you can 450/ write, you can write Teeline' and it is easier to 460/ build speed on outlines which come naturally to mind than 470/ in having to remember suggestions on how to shorten them. 480/

480 words

HINT 6: Speed depends upon instant remembering of outlines, so the more you read and practise writing the words and exercises in this book and in your notebook the faster you will be able to write them and the quicker you will remember them when they occur again. Don't linger over one word when taking notes. If you have not completed it to your satisfaction, leave it and carry on writing. You can fill in any gaps when reading through your notes, and then you will have time to think about any outline you are not happy with and practise it separately.

Teewords : Sample List

In Teeline, when two or more words are represented by a single outline, we call that outline a word-grouping.

The simplest kind of word-grouping consists of two words joined together - it was ⟨outline⟩ , to be ⟨outline⟩ , there were ⟨outline⟩ , and so on.   In cases where several words, or perhaps two polysyllabic words, form a familiar expression, the writer may wish to form a word grouping but, in order to avoid a cumbersome outline, may also need to do a little streamlining.

Various methods of grouping are set out in the textbook TEELINE, Chapter 13 an some methods of contracting groupings in Second Teeline Workbook. The forming of Teewords takes this contraction a step further.   A Teeword is simply a memory aid for a streamlined word-grouping, for example :-

Familiar Expression	Separated Outlines	Cumbersome Word Grouping	Teeword	Teeword Outline
Both sides of industry	⟨outline⟩	⟨outline⟩	Bosindy	⟨outline⟩ or ⟨outline⟩

Understanding this principle will enable the individual Teeline writer to devi his or her own Teewords. Look and listen for a cliche, idiom or hackneyed phrase. Reduce it to its bare essentials, devise your Teeline and construct your outline. The ideal outline is one which gives a speed increase with no loss of readability.

As Teeword outlines are a personalised form of shorthand, the following list merely provides examples - mostly from the world of industrial relations - and should not be regarded as mandatory.

Expression	Teeword	Outline
both sides of industry	bosindy	⟨outline⟩ or ⟨outline⟩
leaders of industry	leadersindy	⟨outline⟩
captains of industry	capsindy	⟨outline⟩
industrial relations	indrations	⟨outline⟩
industrial strife	industrife	⟨outline⟩
industrial action	indaction	⟨outline⟩

Expression	Teeword	Outline
industrial dispute	induspute	
balance of payments	balments	
balance of trade	baltrade	
cost of living	costling	
standard of living	stanling	or
government expenditure	gex/govex	or
government's policy	govcy	
government spending	gosping	
government intervention	govention	
productivity deal	proddle	
self-financing productivity deal	selproddle	
strike action	straction	
selective strike action	selstraction	
average earnings	avernings	
prices and incomes policy	pricomcy	
comparability study	compasty	
free collective bargaining	freecobing	
private sector	prisector	
productivity	prody	
public sector	pusector	
work to rule	worktrule	
secondary picketing	spicketing	
pay negotiations	paynegs	
pay bargaining	pargaining	

Expression	Teeword	Outline
law and order	lawnder	
police officer	pofficer	
demarcation dispute	demardis	

Some of these expressions will appear in some of the following passages.
Look out for them and look them up in this list, when preparing the
passage for dictation.

FACILITY DRILL 56:

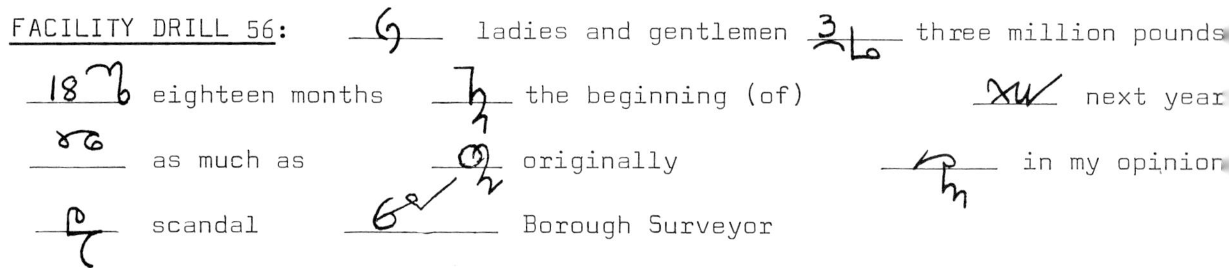

_____ ladies and gentlemen _____ three million pounds 18 _____ eighteen months _____ the beginning (of) _____ next year _____ as much as _____ originally _____ in my opinion _____ scandal _____ Borough Surveyor

PASSAGE 56:

Ladies and gentlemen: When work started on this scheme, two 10 years ago, the
estimated cost was three million pounds. It 20 was also believed that it would
be completed in eighteen 30 months. Now we are told that it will not be 40
completed until the beginning of next year and we have 50 heard that it will
cost twice as much as was 60 originally thought. In my opinion, this is a
scandal and 70 the Borough Surveyor must take his share of the blame.

80 words

FACILITY DRILL 57:

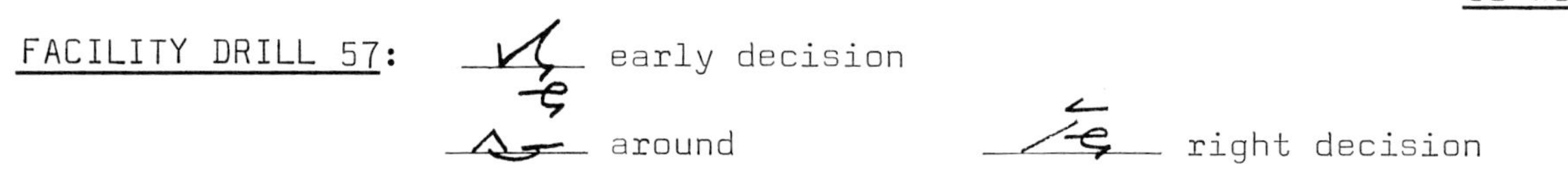

_____ early decision _____ around _____ right decision

PASSAGE 57:

We have been offered two plans for the new town 10 centre and I think either of
them will do. Since 20 there is no pressure on us to come to an 30 early
decision, I maintain we should take our time and 40 make sure we reach the right
decision. Each scheme will 50 cost around a million pounds, which is enough
of a 60 burden on the ratepayers, but if we want a new 70 town centre we must be
prepared to pay for it. 80

80 words

FACILITY DRILL 58:

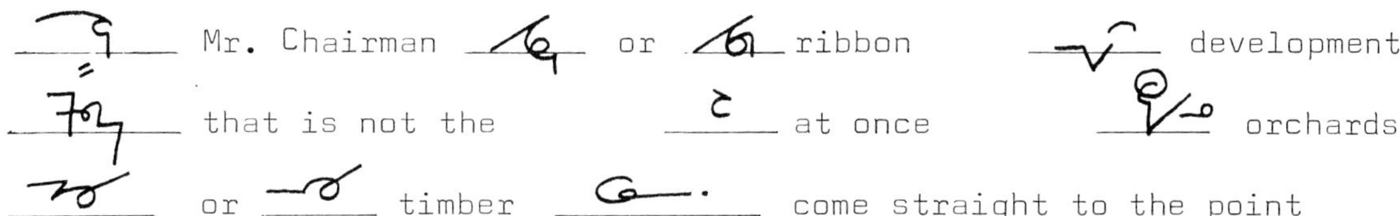

______ Mr. Chairman ______ or ______ ribbon ______ development

______ that is not the ______ at once ______ orchards

______ or ______ timber ______ come straight to the point

PASSAGE 58:

Mr. Chairman, ladies and gentlemen: I will come straight to 10 the point. We must stop this ribbon development at once 20 or we shall find that it is too late to 30 save our town. Many of our finest buildings on the 40 outskirts of the town have already been destroyed and much 50 of our beautiful countryside has disappeared. I can recall the 60 time when this town was surrounded by woods, orchards and 70 open fields. As you all know, that is not the 80 case today. Roads have been built across the fields and 90 nearly all the trees have been chopped down for timber. 100

100 words

FACILITY DRILL 59:

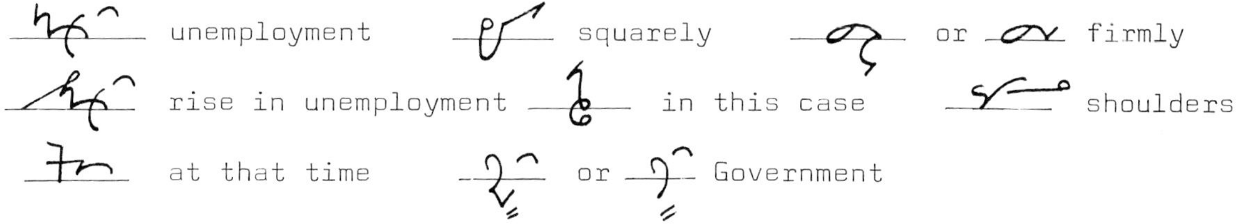

______ unemployment ______ squarely ______ or ______ firmly

______ rise in unemployment ______ in this case ______ shoulders

______ at that time ______ or ______ Government

PASSAGE 59:

I always feel sorry for a Government which cannot cope 10 because of events which are not within its control. In 20 this case, however, it cannot be said that this is 30 true. The blame for the high level of unemployment must 40 rest fairly and squarely on the shoulders of this Government. 50 If they had taken a little more notice of the 60 rise in unemployment last year, and if they had acted 70 firmly at that time, the troubles which face us today 80 could have been avoided. The danger now is that it 90 may be too late to do anything about the problem. 100

100 words

FACILITY DRILL 60:

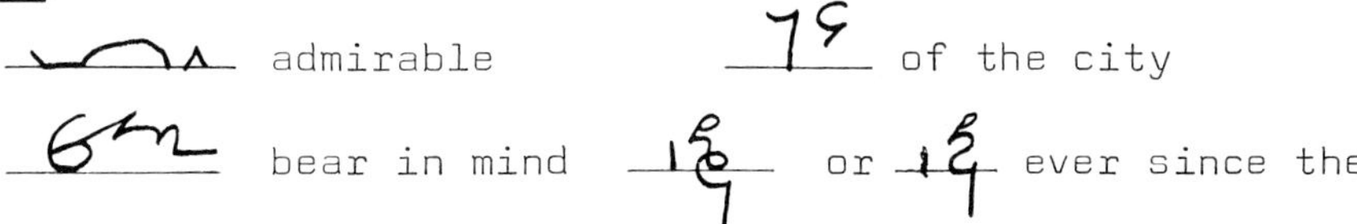

______ admirable ______ of the city

______ bear in mind ______ or ______ ever since the

PASSAGE 60:

Ladies and gentlemen: We have been asked to consider the /⁰proposal that this
area of waste ground to the south /⁰of the city should be developed as a
housing estate./⁰ There has been a need for more houses in that /⁰district for
some time: in fact, ever since the new /⁰factories were built on London Road.
In itself, therefore, this /⁰is an admirable idea, but what we have to bear /⁰
in mind is whether, in these days of rising costs, /⁰it makes economic sense
to spend a considerable sum of /⁰money in this particular way. I think it
does not./⁰   100 words

FACILITY DRILL 61:   ___ according (to)   ___ thirty-thousand

___ architectural   ___ in danger of   ___ state of affairs

___ important part   ___ some of them   ___ derelict

PASSAGE 61:

According to a recent report, about thirty thousand buildings in /⁰Britain
which are of historical or architectural interest are in /⁰danger of becoming
derelict.   The reasons for this sorry state /⁰of affairs are many. In some
cases, the owners do /⁰not have the necessary financial resources to maintain
their properties./⁰ In other cases, vandals have caused considerable damage to
empty /⁰buildings. Whatever the reasons, there is no doubt that the /⁰people
of Britain are in danger of losing an important /⁰part of their national
heritage, even if some of them /⁰are not aware of it and others do not care./⁰

FACILITY DRILL 62:

___ this council   ___ has said   ___ or ___ abused

___ sort of thing   ___ town council

PASSAGE 62:

Mr. Chairman: While not agreeing with all that the previous /⁰speaker has
said, it is my opinion that she spoke /⁰a lot of good sense. For example, I
am in /⁰complete agreement with her when she says that this council /⁰should
build its own houses and not contract the work /⁰out to local builders. There
is no doubt that the /⁰system of asking for tenders from builders has been

much $\int^{70}$ abused in the past and on more than one occasion $\int^{80}$ the good name of the council has been dragged in $\int^{90}$ the dust of scandal. To stop that sort of thing $\int^{100}$ happening again would be a good reason on its $\int^{110}$ own for the town council to build its own houses. $\int^{120}$ 120 words

FACILITY DRILL 63: (See General Note on dates & figures following Introduction.)

or proceedings	equip	budget
two point eight million pounds	half a million pounds *	
in other words	how much	tennis
activities (See P.29, Second Teeline Workbook for the 'tivity' ending.)		

(* might be read back as 6 million, if the F loop were badly written.
    The insertion of A makes this outline safer.)

PASSAGE 63:

The purpose of these proceedings is to decide how we $\int^{10}$ can equip this new sports centre with the limited amount $\int^{20}$ of money available. As you know, it cost two point $\int^{30}$ eight million pounds to build. That means that we cannot $\int^{40}$ afford to spend more than half a million pounds on $\int^{50}$ equipment because we have to keep within the original budget $\int^{60}$ of three point three million pounds. Our task at this $\int^{70}$ meeting is to share out five hundred thousand pounds among $\int^{80}$ the various sporting activities. In other words, we have to $\int^{90}$ decide how much money to spend on football, how much $\int^{100}$ on tennis, and so on. It will not be an $\int^{110}$ easy task, but it is one we must accomplish today. $\int^{120}$

                                                    120 words

FACILITY DRILL 64: like to say   to say   superb
compliments   appreciation   superfluous

PASSAGE 64:

Ladies and gentlemen: I should like to say how much $\int^{10}$ I have enjoyed myself as your guest this evening. In $\int^{20}$ fact, it would not be going too far to say $\int^{30}$ that this has been the most enjoyable evening of the $\int^{40}$ year for me. Certainly, I am sure you will all $\int^{50}$ agree with me that the dinner was superb and I $\int^{60}$ hope you will pass on my compliments to those who $\int^{70}$ were responsible for it.   We have already shown our appreciation [80] of the entertainers who amused us after dinner and any [90] further words from me would be superfluous. Once again, I [100] thank you, ladies and gentlemen, and I hope the coming [110] year will be a very successful one for your society. [120]

<u>120 words</u>

FACILITY DRILL 65:

about time   beating about the bush   replaced   overdue   demolished   ancient   perspective

PASSAGE 65:

Ladies and gentlemen: I think it is about time we [10] put this matter into its proper perspective. All we seem [20] to have done so far is to generate a lot [30] of hot air and if we want to get anywhere [40] we shall have to stop beating about the bush. We [50] are here to consider the proposal that our old town [60] hall should be pulled down and replaced by a new [70] office block. Now, to my way of thinking this is [80] an excellent idea. Indeed, I would say that it is [90] an idea which is at least ten years overdue. The [100] old town hall is just one of many ancient buildings [110] in this town which should have been demolished long ago. [120]

<u>120 words</u>

FACILITY DRILL 66:

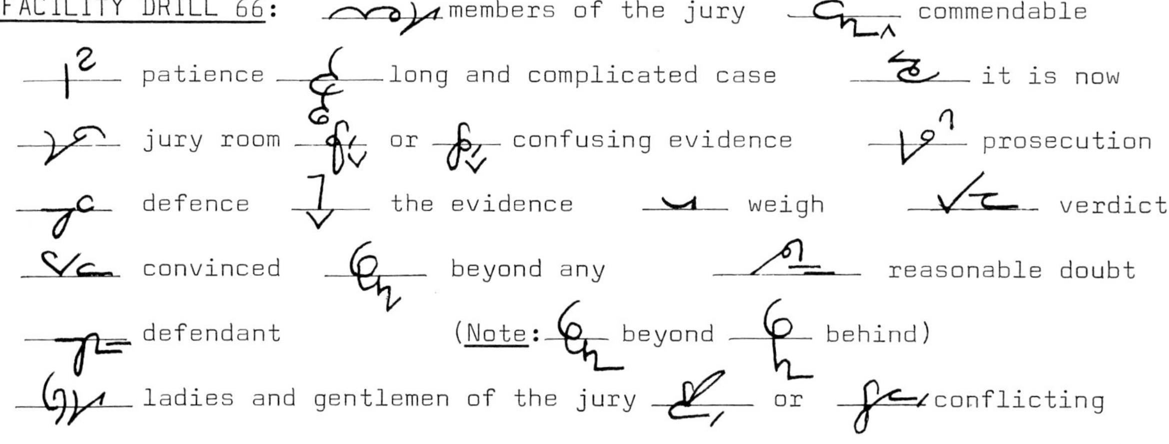

members of the jury   commendable   patience   long and complicated case   it is now   jury room   or   confusing evidence   prosecution   defence   the evidence   weigh   verdict   convinced   beyond any   reasonable doubt   defendant   (<u>Note</u>: beyond   behind)   ladies and gentlemen of the jury   or   conflicting

PASSAGE 66:

Members of the Jury: You have listened with commendable patience / to a long [10] and complicated case and it is now [20] your duty to retire to the jury room in order [30] to consider the arguments you have heard during the past [40] five weeks. In many ways, this has been a difficult [50] case in which a lot of conflicting and confusing evidence 60 has been presented by both the prosecution and the defence. 70 Nevertheless, it is your responsibility, ladies and gentlemen of the 80 jury, to weigh the evidence for and against the accused 90 and to arrive at a just verdict. Finally, I must 100 remind you that unless you are convinced beyond any reasonable 110 doubt that the defendant committed the crime of which he 120 stands accused, then he must not be found guilty. Throughout 130 your deliberations you must remember those two words – 'reasonable doubt'. 140

140 words

FACILITY DRILL 67:

draw your attention   Treasurer's   show of hands

PASSAGE 67:

Ladies and gentlemen: May I draw your attention to our 10 Treasurer's report. Although the financial position is very good, there 20 are signs that if we are not able to attract 30 more new members during the coming year, the affairs of 40 the Society will take a turn for the worse. I 50 feel that we should be doing our best to get 60 as many new members as we can and I should 70 like, therefore, to put to you the idea of a 80 recruiting drive. Before I go into details, however, I should 90 like to know whether or not there is general support 100 for the idea. Perhaps the best thing to do is 110 to have an open discussion on the matter and then, 120 after perhaps ten minutes or so, to have a show 130 of hands to see if it is worth serious consideration. 140

140 words

FACILITY DRILL 68:

like to see   after all

citizens   redevelopment   tolerant

slow off the mark   it is their

PASSAGE 68:

Mr. Chairman: I should like to see this matter handled 10 in a different way. I think the ratepayers should be 20 given an opportunity to express their views. After all, it 30 is their money which we are proposing to spend and, 40 as the previous speaker pointed out, we have to be 50 very careful in these days when it comes to spending 60 ratepayers' money. The citizens of this town are never slow 70 off the mark when it comes to organising protest meetings [80] and the last thing we want is a repeat of [90] what happened two years ago when we tried to rush [100] through the redevelopment scheme for the indoor market. It is [110] not likely that the ratepayers would be any more tolerant [120] as far as the present proposal is concerned unless the [130] entire scheme is explained to them at a public meeting. [140]   <u>140 words</u>

FACILITY DRILL 69:

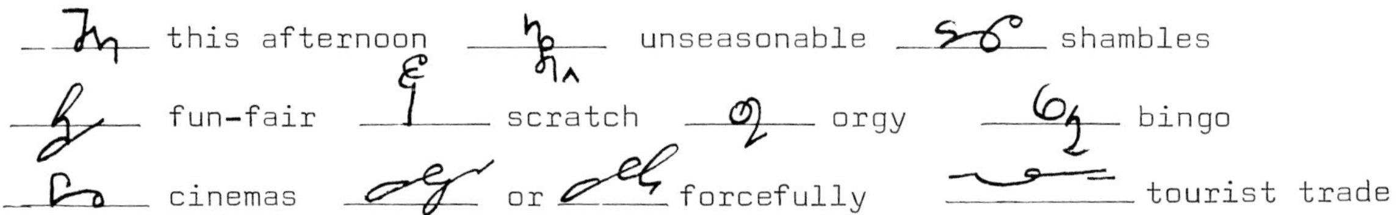

this afternoon	unseasonable	shambles
fun-fair	scratch	orgy	bingo
cinemas	or forcefully	tourist trade

PASSAGE 69:

I have come here this afternoon to address members of [10] this council on the terrible state of the amenities in [20] the town. Due to the unseasonable weathe of last summer [30] the entire promenade is a shambles and the damage to [40] the fun-fair on the pier was so severe that [50] it will probably have to be rebuilt from scratch. The [60] weather was not the only factor in this orgy of [70] destruction. I need hardly remind you that our town was [80] visited by vandals on several occasions last summer and they [90] caused a great deal of damage, particularly to the cinemas [100] and bingo halls. The point I wish to make most[1] forcefully is that it is high time this council set [120] about the job of repairing the damage or there will [130] be very little tourist trade in this town next summer. [140]   <u>140 words</u>

FACILITY DRILL 70:

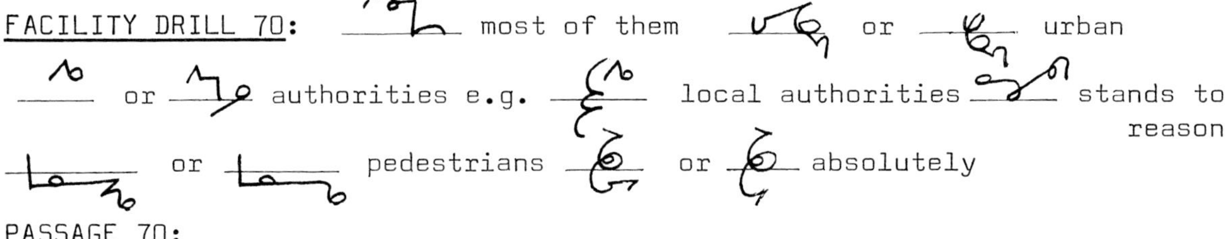

most of them	or	urban
or authorities e.g.	local authorities	stands to reason
or pedestrians	or	absolutely

PASSAGE 70:

This is good news, ladies and gentlemen. We have been [10] saying for many years that all vehicles should be banned [20] in the town centre. Now, at last, it seems that [30] the council has come round to our way of thinking. [40] Towns are made by people for people and that is [50] something which has been forgotten by most local authorities ever 60 since the motor car was invented. Almost seven hundred people 70 are killed every month on Britain's roads and most of 80 them meet their doom in urban areas. It stands to 90 reason that cars, lorries and motor cycles should not be 100 allowed in crowded shopping areas. Our town is especially dangerous 110 for pedestrians because our streets are old and narrow with 120 dozens of blind corners. They are simply not made for 130 cars and lorries and I am absolutely delighted that the 140 council has at last decided to tackle this grave problem. 150   150 words

FACILITY DRILL 71:

Residents' Association   or   proximity   convey

PASSAGE 71:

As a member of the Residents' Association, I feel very 10 strongly that our official representatives should convey our views to 20 the Council. It is quite clear that there is not 30 a single member who supports the council's plan to build 40 houses on this plot of land at the edge of 50 our estate and we must do all we can to 60 put a stop to this stupid idea. We have all 70 paid good money for the privilege of living on a 80 private estate and I for one am not going to 90 stand by and watch the value of my house go 100 down because of its proximity to a cluster of council 110 houses. I know we shall be accused of snobbery, but 120 what I have said about the falling value of our 130 houses is the truth and if we can stop that 140 happening then we should not worry about being called snobs. 150   150 words

FACILITY DRILL 72:

thousands of millions of pounds   annual trade deficit

financial crisis   general election   in fact

they would   20/ twenty per cent   of the kind

latest figures   or   before very long   immediate action

PASSAGE 72:

I am of the opinion that before very long government 10 spending will reach an all-time high. Indeed, I would 20 go so far as to say that unless immediate action [30] is taken to curtail expenditure in the <u>public sector</u>, this [40] country will find itself in the red to the tune [50] of thousands of millions of pounds. Our annual trade deficit [60] is already running at three hundred million pounds and it [70] is quite clear that we cannot continue to live beyond [80] our means. During last year's general election campaign the government [90] promised that if they were re-elected they would cut <u>government [100] expenditure</u> but they have done nothing of the kind. In [110] fact, the latest figures show an increase of twenty per [120] cent over last year's figure. There is no doubt that [130] unless immediate action is taken, this country will find itself [140] with its biggest financial crisis for at least forty years. [150]

<u>150 words</u>

<u>NOTE</u>: The phrases underlined in the passage above and in subsequent passages will be found in the list of TEEWORDS on Page 54.

FACILITY DRILL 73:

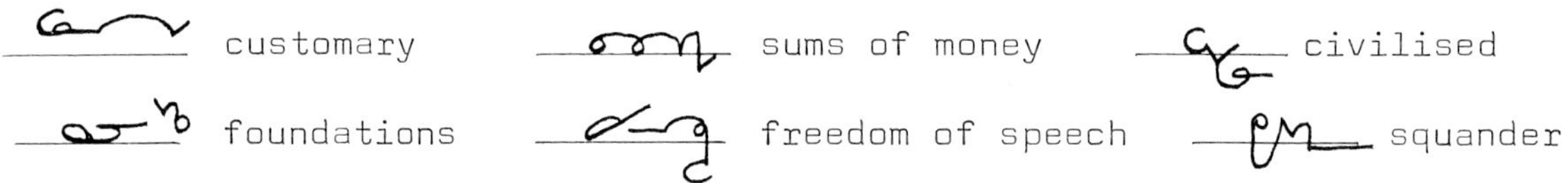

customary   sums of money   civilised

foundations   freedom of speech   squander

PASSAGE 73:

Mr. Chairman and Fellow Members: We are here tonight to [10] debate the proposition that this Society should donate six hundred [20] pounds to the church restoration fund. Now it is not [30] customary for this Society to donate large sums of money [40] for such purposes and I do not think this is [50] the right time for us to depart from our usual [60] practice. For some time I have been intending to speak [70] out against those misguided people who seem determined to destroy [80] the very foundations on which our Society was built, but [90] I have always said to myself that freedom of speech [100] is one of the most important liberties of civilised life, [110] and, however much one may disagree with other's opinions, their [120] right to express them must be respected. Tonight, however, I [130] have decided that the time has come when I must [140] speak out against those foolish people who would have us [150] squander our funds on an old church that no-one attends. [160]

<u>160 words</u>

FACILITY DRILL 74:

<table>
<tr><td>_____________ sooner the better</td><td>_______ ruining (_______ = running)</td></tr>
<tr><td>_______ up and up</td><td>_______ down and down</td></tr>
</table>

PASSAGE 74:

Ladies and gentlemen: In my opinion we need a return /10 to _free collective bargaining_ in this country, and the sooner /20 the better. It is the only way to do away /30 with the _industrial strife_ which is ruining our country. _Free_ /40 _collective bargaining_ is what _both sides of industry_ want. In /50 recent years, _productivity deals_, particularly _self-financing productivity deals_, have /60 been a major part of the Government's _prices and incomes_ /70 _policy_ but the _cost of living_ has gone up and /80 up while the average worker's _standard of living_ has gone /90 down and down. _Government intervention_ in _pay bargaining_ has been /100 the direct cause of _strike action_ on numerous occasions when /110 employers have not been allowed to award pay rises which /120 they would otherwise have been happy to award. Even the /130 _leaders of industry_ have gone on record as saying that /140 many _industrial disputes_ would not have occured if only the /150 system of _free collective bargaining_ had been allowed to operate. /160

160 words

FACILITY DRILL 75:

<table>
<tr><td>_______ honoured</td><td>_______ daunting</td><td>_______ charity</td></tr>
<tr><td>_______ without saying</td><td>_______ or _______ festive</td><td></td></tr>
</table>

PASSAGE 75:

Ladies: It goes without saying that I am very pleased /10 to be here on this festive occasion. I must also /20 say how very honoured I felt when I received your /30 invitation. It was the first time I had ever been /40 asked to make the opening speech at such an event /50 and I must admit I did find the prospect a /60 little daunting. However, I accepted the invitation without hesitation, and /70 I am very glad that I did. After all, it /80 is not every day that I get the chance to /90 sample dozens of home-made cakes and wines. Before we /100 all start to enjoy ourselves, though, I should like to[110] remind you that all the proceeds of this day will[120] go to charity, so this is an ideal opportunity to[130] spend more than you can afford without feeling too guilty.[140] It gives me the very greatest pleasure, as your honoured[150] guest, to declare that this festive event is now open.[160]

160 words

FACILITY DRILL 76:

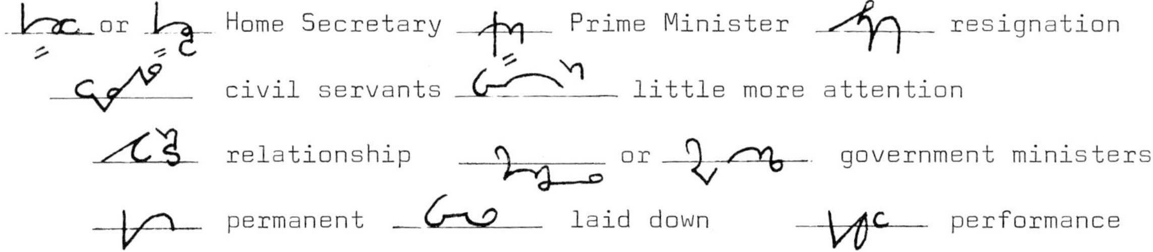

or   Home Secretary   Prime Minister   resignation

civil servants   little more attention

relationship   or   government ministers

permanent   laid down   performance

PASSAGE 76:

It is always a sad day for the government when[10] a Minister has to resign. It is also a sad[20] day for the whole country when, as in this case,[30] he had always done his best for the country. The[40] Home Secretary has had to hand in his resignation because[50] of the actions of his civil servants. That is a[60] great pity, because he has done a good job while[70] he has been in office. Indeed, if the Prime Minister[80] and the rest of the Cabinet had paid a little[90] more attention to what he was telling them six months[100] ago about the power of some senior civil servants he[110] would never have been placed in such an impossible position.[120]

This whole affair raises some important questions about the relationship[130] between government ministers and their permanent civil servants. I think[140] some clear guidelines need to be laid down on that[150] relationship before we have a repeat performance and yet another[160] Minister has to go.   164 words

FACILITY DRILL 77:   or   fingertips   salient

function   maximum   or   efficiency

moreover   fickle   basis   court reporting

consequences   plea   weighty   anywhere else

substantial   guilty   not guilty

PASSAGE 77:

The newspaper reporter with no shorthand is unable to function /10 with maximum efficienty. Moreover, he is likely to make mistakes /20 which could turn out to be costly, both for himself /30 and his paper. Without a reliable note, he has to /40 rely on memory and we all know how fickle our /50 memory can be. The reliable shorthand record forms the basis /60 of a journalist's defence to the charge of misreporting what /70 someone actually said and it is surprising how often that /80 charge is made. Perhaps the value of an accurate note /90 is greater in court reporting than anywhere else, because the /100 consequences of making an error can be extremely serious. Simple /110 mistakes such as confusing a plea of not guilty with /120 one of guilty can result in a claim for substantial /130 damages being brought against a newspaper. Such weighty matters apart, /140 the shorthand note is an invaluable aid to writing up /150 a story. When all the salient facts, plus a few /160 good quotes, are literally at the writer's fingertips the story /170 should almost write itself.

174 words

FACILITY DRILL 78:

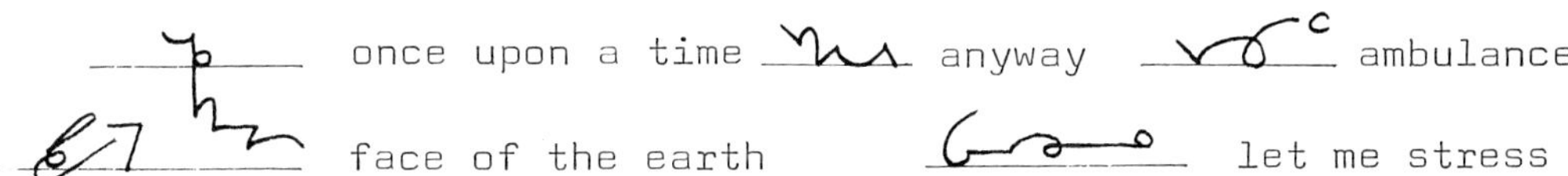

once upon a time   anyway   ambulance

face of the earth   let me stress

PASSAGE 78:

Ladies and gentlemen, let me tell you a little story. /10 Once upon a time, not so very long ago, in /20 fact, there lived in this town a certain Mr. Smith. /30 He was thirty-three years old, married with two young /40 children. In short, he was an average citizen, hard-working /50 and law-abiding apart from the occasional brush with a /60 traffic warden. Anyway, one dark November evening, Mr. Smith left /70 his semi-detached house and started to walk towards the /80 Rose and Crown public house in Park Road. It was /90 a very short journey, a journey he had made on /100 many occasions, for he was partial to a pint of /110 bitter after a day's work as an ambulance driver. This /120 time, however, he did not arrive at the pub for /130 his pint of beer. Where he did go is still /140 a complete mystery, because Mr. Smith has not been seen /150 from that day to this. Apparently, he simply disappeared from /160 the face of the earth.   Let me stress, ladies and [170] gentlemen, that this man disappeared without reason, that he took [180] nothing with him beyond what he needed for his usual [190] trip to the Rose and Crown in nearby Park Road. [200]

200 words

FACILITY DRILL 79:

_______ lawyers   _______ Crown   _______ or _______ nutshell   _______ factual

_______ balanced   _______ impartial   _______ its decision   _______ usable

_______ knowledgeable   _______ layman

PASSAGE 79:

Journalists do not have to be lawyers, but they must [10] be aware of what they can and cannot do when [20] reporting a trial.   The accused is entitled to a fair [30] trial and that means that court copy must be looked [40] at, both from the point of view of the Crown [50] and that of the person in the dock. In a [60] nutshell, it must be factual, impartial and balanced. A reporter [70] may sometimes have a great deal of inside knowledge about [80] a crime, but once a person is to face the [90] court accused of that crime, then most of that knowledge [100] will have to go under the counter.

When the jury [110] has reached its decision the reporter has further thinking to [120] do. If the verdict is guilty, then most of that [130] inside information will probably be usable. If, however, the verdict [140] is not guilty then the reporter may have to sit [150] on his inside information for the rest of his life [160] because he now has material which, if published, could form [170] the basis of an action for libel.   A journalist may [180] not have to be a lawyer but in certain areas [190] of the law he cannot afford to be anything other [200] than a very knowledgeable layman.

205 words

FACILITY DRILL 80:

_______ fabric   _______ High Court   _______ in our   _______ Crown Courts

_______ or _______ County Courts   _______ or _______ Magistrates Courts

_______ magistrates   _______ abandoned   _______ husband   _______ or _______ upkeep

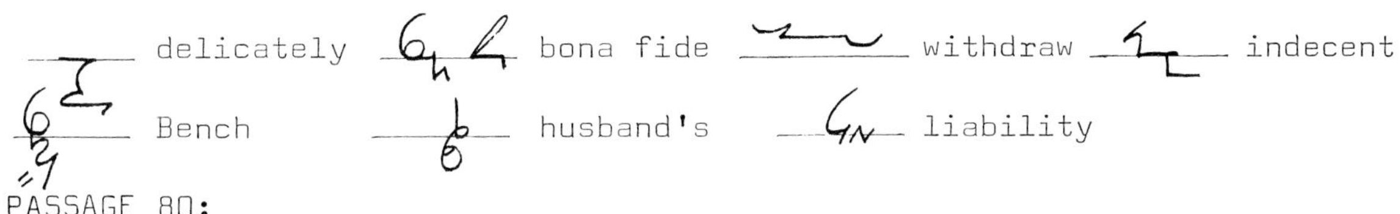

PASSAGE 80:

The family is a vital thread in the fabric of [10]our society and because of its importance there is a [20]branch of the law which is devoted to family affairs. [30] This is the Family Division of the High Court, centred [40]on London but active throughout the country in our Crown [50]Courts, County Courts and Magistrates Courts.   Much of the work [60]load in family affairs is borne by local magistrates and [70]the cases they hear are known as domestic cases.   A [80]wife abandoned by her husband may appear before the Bench [90]asking for an order to be made in respect of [100]her departed husband's liability to pay for the upkeep of [110]his family.   A wife who no longer wishes to live [120]with her husband may apply for a separation order and, [130] if it is granted, the magistrates have the power to [140]order that any children of the marriage shall be taken [150]into the care of the local authority, should they think [160]this advisable. Such matters must be handled somewhat delicately, so [170]members of the general public are not allowed to sit [180]in court when these cases are being heard.   Bona fide [190]reporters have the right to do so and very often [200]some good stories come from domestic proceedings.   In certain cases, [210]however, even the press may be asked to withdraw.   This [220]occurs most often when evidence of an indecent nature is [230]about to be given.   234 words

FACILITY DRILL 81:

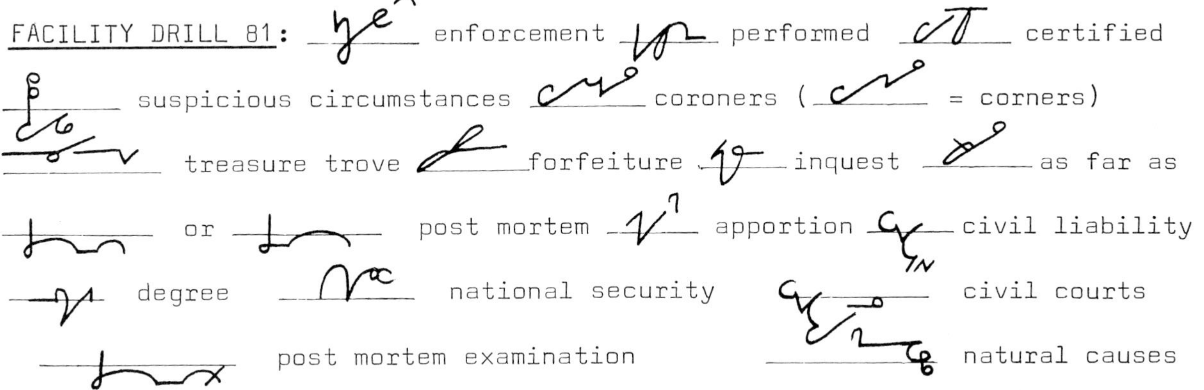

PASSAGE 81:

Although in days gone by the coroner performed certain law 10 enforcement duties, today his main functions are to determine the 20 cause of a person's death when it cannot immediately be 30 certified as due to natural causes and to inquire into 40 deaths which occur under suspicious circumstances. However, coroners do have 50 another duty, and that is to determine whether buried treasure 60 is owned by someone or is treasure trove and therefore 70 subject to forfeiture to the Crown.

In any event, whether 80 it be a dead body or buried treasure, the coroner 90 holds an inquiry which is known as an inquest. As 100 far as journalists are concerned, the important point is that 110 every inquest must be held in public and can be 120 reported unless the coroner decides that a private hearing is 130 necessary in the interests of national security. Not every suspicious 140 death will lead to an inquest, for after the coroner 150 has ordered a post-mortem examination it may be found 160 that death was, in fact, due to natural causes. In 170 such a situation, an inquest will be waived and the 180 coroner's office will notify the Press accordingly.

More often than 190 not, a coroner will sit with a jury who will 200 return a verdict, but such cases are not trials. It 210 is no part of such proceedings to apportion any degree 220 of civil liability for any death. The inquest is to 230 determine the exact circumstances of death and it would be 240 a matter for the civil courts to decide on, for 250 example, the question of damages resulting from a road accident. 260

<u>260 words</u>

FACILITY DRILL 82:

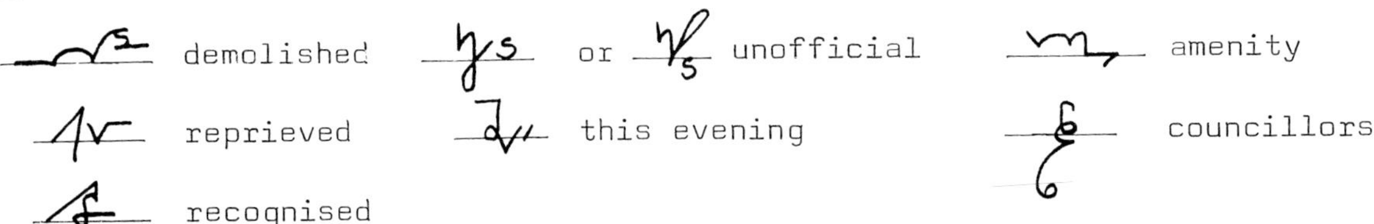

demolished or unofficial amenity

reprieved this evening councillors

recognised

<u>NOTE</u>: The following symbols can be used with safety in context :-

top right hand corner top left hand corner

bottom right hand corner bottom left hand corner

PASSAGE 82:

As you all know, the purpose of this meeting is [10] to discuss the Council's proposal that the old clinic at [20] the top right-hand corner of the market place should [30] be pulled down. That is the main item on the [40] agenda and it is important that we determine our opinions [50] on that before we move on to the question of [60] what should be built in place of the clinic. After [70] all, if we decide that the clinic should not be [80] demolished, then we shall take our stand on that and [90] the question of what should be built to replace it [100] will not arise.   On the other hand, if we decide [110] that it should come down, we have to consider [120] the Council's idea of allowing a super-market on the site. [130] First things first, however. Two years ago, when this matter [140] was first raised, the arguments in favour of retaining the [150] old clinic centred on its value as a building of [160] historic interest. You may recall, ladies and gentlemen, that an [170] attempt was made to have it officially recognised as such, [180] but the application was turned down. That seemed to be [190] the end of the matter until we heard from an [200] unofficial source that if some use could be found for [210] the building - a use which could be regarded as a [220] public amenity - then the building might well be reprieved.

Our [230] task this evening is to decide if the old clinic [240] is a suitable place for a genuine social activity. If [250] so, then we must make public our opposition to the [260] council's plan and canvass our local councillors for their support. [270]

270 words

FACILITY DRILL 83:

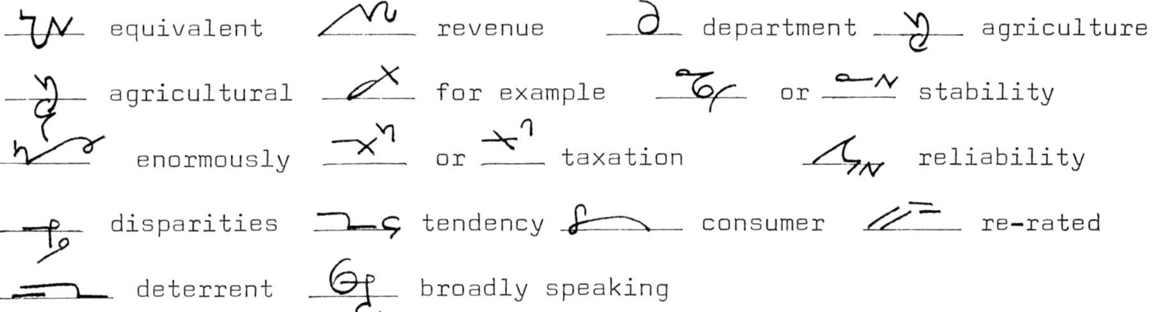

PASSAGE 83:

Rates are a form of property tax. Broadly speaking, the amount of rates paid reflects the value of the property. In Britain, the basis of valuation is known as annual rental value, which is equivalent to the rent which might reasonably be expected to be received in a year if the property were let on a free market. It is not generally known, that since nineteen-forty-eight, the Inland Revenue, a department of central government, has been responsible for the valuation of all property for rating purposes. The local authority determines the level of rate to be levied. Certain types of property may be partially or totally exempt from paying rates: for example, churches, agricultural buildings and public parks. Income from the rates is enormously important to local authorities. It is the major local tax and is the main source of revenue over which they have control. There are several merits of rates as a form of taxation. They are easy to assess, cheap to collect, simple to administer and possess stability and reliability as a source of income. Rates are, however, a much criticised tax. In the first place, because it is an impersonal tax, ability to pay is not related to income although rebates can be obtained by the less well-off citizens. Secondly, there are disparities in the levies imposed by different local authorities on similar properties. Thirdly, there is a tendency for any rises in the rates for commercial and industrial properties to be passed on to the consumer in the form of higher prices for products. Fourthly, an improved property is re-rated at a higher value which acts as a deterrent to the houseowner or landlord who might otherwise be willing to carry out improvements such as building a garage or installing central heating.

300 words

FACILITY DRILL 84:   council's decision   High Street   or   ascertain   how many more people   no evidence   or   ingrained   or   woo   retrograde   suburbs   youngsters   or   playgrounds [shorthand] ratepayers   [shorthand] thereby   [shorthand] cultural life

[shorthand] multi-storey   [shorthand] unfortunate decision.

PASSAGE 84:

Ladies and gentlemen: In my opinion the council's decision to [10] provide a multi-storey car park behind the High Street [20] is absolutely deplorable. If there is one thing which this [30] town does not need then it is a multi-storey [40] car park. It has been argued that the provision of [50] the car park will attract more shoppers to the town [60] and so lead to greater prosperity for all who live [70] here, but I must register my strong disagreement with that [80] line of argument. In the first place, insufficient research has [90] been done in order to ascertain just how many more [100] people will come into town to do their shopping simply [110] because we have a multi-storey car park. In this [120] area shopping habits are deeply ingrained and there is no [130] evidence to support the view that we can woo people [140] away from other towns where they already have their favourite [150] shops. What will happen, in my view, is that house-wives [160] who live in the suburbs and who, at the moment, [170] come into town by public transport, will start to use [180] their cars instead. This will lead to an increase in [190] the already serious congestion in the centre of the town. [200] For that reason I feel that building this car park [210] would turn out to be a retrograde step and not [220] a progressive one. To my mind, we should be using [230] available space in the town to provide facilities which would [240] cater for the cultural life of the town. We need [250] a new indoor swimming pool, an exhibition hall, a new [260] theatre and several adventure playgrounds for our youngsters. Any one [270] of these would be better than a multi-storey car [280] park and would probably cost the ratepayer a lot less. [290] It should be our aim, ladies and gentlemen, to reduce [300] the number of vehicles in the town centre, and therefore [310] make it a safer and more peaceful place. I suggest [320] we petition the council to reverse this most unfortunate decision. [330]   <u>330 words</u>

FACILITY DRILL 85:

[shorthand] some of them   [shorthand] few of them   [shorthand] necessity   [shorthand] far cry

[shorthand] homeless people   [shorthand] vast majority   [shorthand] derelict

74

or pence cup of tea of our society

soup single people canvas down and outs

<u>PASSAGE 85</u>:

Ladies and gentlemen: I wish to draw your attention to 10 what I consider to
be a very serious problem. Every 20 night, in this town, at least one hundred
people sleep 30 rough. Some of them, very few of them, in fact, 40 do so from
choice, but for the vast majority it 50 is a matter of necessity. We often
hear the term 60 'homeless people' but I wonder how many of us have 70 given
any real thought to what that really means. I 80 suppose that most of us have,
at one time or 90 another, spent the odd night in the open air, perhaps 100 after
missing the last train home. Some of us may 110 have spent several weeks under
canvas, either as a holiday 120 or as part of a training scheme. But such
experiences 130 are a far cry from what I mean by 'sleeping 140 rough'.
In this town there are people who have spent 150 every night for ten or twenty
years sleeping in derelict 160 buildings with only rats for company. In the
daytime they 170 wander around the town looking for scraps of food and 180 trying
to beg a few pence for a cup of 190 tea.   Quite frequently they resort to shop-
lifting and who 200 can blame them? The worst that can happen to them 210 if they
get caught is to be sent to prison 220 and that means a considerable rise in
their <u>standard of 230 living</u>.
These people are the lepers of our society, ladies 240 and gentlemen. There are
a few charitable organisations which try 250 to help by providing soup runs and
hostel accommodation, but 260 most of us either do not know about the problem 270
or choose to forget about it.   It might be thought 280 that these unfortunates
would get special consideration as far as 290 housing is concerned but that is
the reverse of the 300 truth. The housing needs of single people have never
been 310 an important part of the council's housing policy and in 320 any case,
these down-and-outs are in a 'catch 330 twenty-two' situation. Because they
have no fixed address they 340 cannot be placed on the housing list. It is
this 350 aspect of the problem that I wish to consider tonight. 360   <u>360 words</u>

<u>FACILITY DRILL 86</u>: nevertheless Welfare State

voluntary society yesteryear ain't

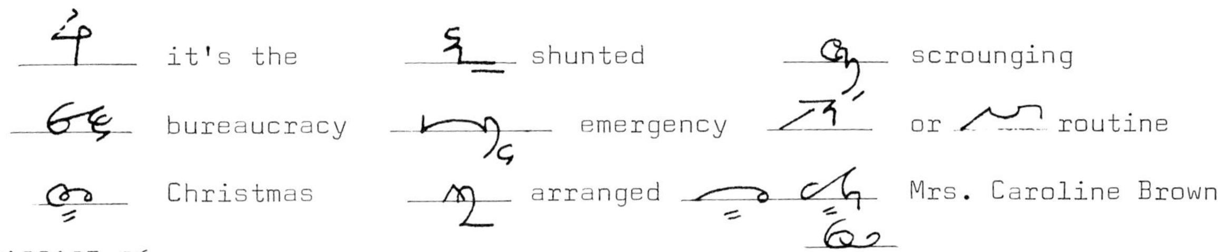

PASSAGE 86:

Ladies and gentlemen: It gives me the greatest possible pleasure to make this introductory speech. I do not want to take up too much of your valuable time, because I know you did not come here tonight to listen to me but to listen to our guest speaker. Nevertheless, I must take this opportunity to review the work of the Society over the past year. In these days, when the Welfare State is an accepted part of everyone's life, it is easy to forget that there are still many people who need the kind of help which a voluntary society such as ours can give. We should always bear in mind that the way we do our work is at least as important as what we do. To quote the words of a popular song of yesteryear: 'It ain't what you do, it's the way that you do it.' The trouble with the Welfare State is that it is too impersonal and too rigid in its administration. The person who needs help quickly is too often shunted from one civil servant to another and from one department to another before any help is given. There is also a great deal of form filling. No doubt, it is necessary. Records have to be kept and scrounging has to be stopped, but it all takes far too much time. In contrast to all this bureaucracy, we act immediately. We visit people in their homes and we give them what they need without asking them to fill in a single form. In addition to providing an emergency service we do a lot of routine charity work and it is here that the personal touch is so valuable. Last year, during the festive season, we gave away three hundred and fifty Christmas puddings and two hundred and thirty pounds in cash to the poor people of this town. During the summer, we arranged coach trips to the seaside for no fewer than one hundred and forty elderly people. But to my mind, one of our most worthwhile activities is simply visiting lonely people in their homes for a chat and a cup of tea. Now that is a service which the Welfare State does not provide, although it is one which is most appreciated[380] by people living alone. It is now my very pleasant[390] duty to introduce our special guest speaker, Mrs. Caroline Brown.[400]

400 words

FACILITY DRILL 87:   _____ requisite   _____ temperament   _____ unlikely (note _____ = unlucky)   _____ or _____ intelligence   _____ hard of hearing   _____ or _____ normally   _____ transcribed   _____ transcript   _____ acute   _____ or _____ intense   _____ perseverance   _____ knowledge of words

PASSAGE 87:   What makes a good shorthand writer?

The first requisite of a good shorthand writer is undoubtedly[10] a thorough knowledge of the system being used and the[20] ability to reach a high speed in that system. That,[30] in itself, will depend partly on the writer's level of[40] intelligence, since a person of low intelligence is unlikely to[50] be able to master this kind of skill; but much[60] depends, too, on a person's temperament. High-speed writers tend[70] to be quick-moving, quick-thinking people. But speed alone[80] is not enough. Many quick-moving, quick-thinking people fail[90] to reach the level of concentration which is necesaary if[100] a complete and accurate note is to be achieved. It[110] is possible, too, that a person with all the above[120] qualifications may be hard-of-hearing, in which case, not[130] everything will be heard, even though he listens intently. Others,[140] although normally able to concentrate upon the matter in hand,[150] may be distracted by sudden noises or movements while taking[160] the note and miss a few words. So, the shorthand[170] writer must be able to keep calm in all circumstances.[180]

To sum up, a good shorthand writer requires acute hearing,[190] intense concentration and a thorough mastery of the skill. Then[200] of course, the note must be transcribed and here the[210] writer's command of language and knowledge of words are important[220] factors. There is little point in taking a complete and[230] accurate note without the ability to make a complete and[240] accurate transcript of it.

It will be seen, therefore, that[250] becoming a good shorthand writer is no easy matter, and [260] to achieve success in this field is an indication of [270] an individual's determination and perseverance, as well as the possession [280] of the other qualities already listed.

286 words

FACILITY DRILL 88:

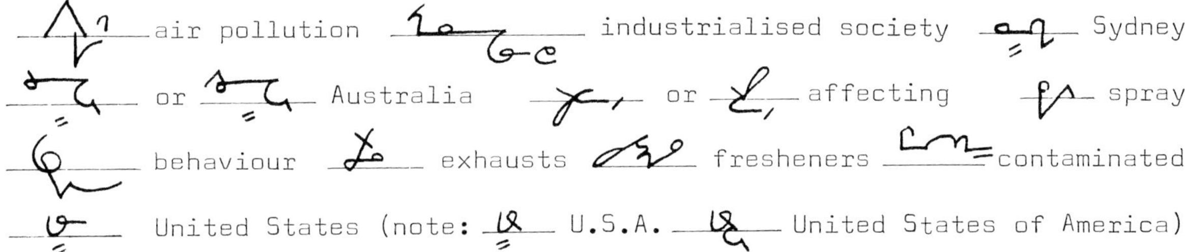

PASSAGE 88: Air Pollution

Amongst the dangers of living in an industrialised society is [10] that of air pollution. The more traffic there is on [20] the roads, the greater the risk, especially if that traffic [30] is moving on petrol power, because petrol contains lead.

A [40] study undertaken in Australia revealed that in Sydney, the high [50] level of lead in the air was affecting children's behaviour. [60] Children who were reported by teachers to be behaving badly [70] were found to have high lead levels in their blood. [80]

For some years now, it has been known that the [90] fumes from car exhausts caused pollution and made some people [100] ill. Those who live in large cities are more at [110] risk than those living in country areas and in many [120] countries, the lead content of petrol has been reduced. Unfortunately, [130] Britain lags well behind the United States and Japan in [140] this respect.

Another study, carried out in Leeds, showed that [150] school children, playing near a main road, not only breathed [160] in lead fumes from passing traffic, and had lead deposited [170] on their hair and clothing, but that it also contaminated [180] the sweets they had been given to carry as part [190] of their experiment. If the children had eaten these sweets, [200] they would have absorbed a much greater amount of lead [210] than that considered to be safe.

It has also been [220] discovered that the use of air fresheners can make some [230] people ill. Recent reports from doctors say that some patients [240] have

experienced strange changes of mood, which disappeared when the air
fresheners were removed from their houses. So, next time you are tempted
to reach for that sweet-smelling spray, think again.   You may be adding
to the pollution by using it, and putting your own health at risk while
doing so.   292 words

FACILITY DRILL 89:

conservative   acknowledge   younger members

non-stop   high-light   pottery

disaster   Midsummer's Day   special committee

our ability   competitors   or   August

I am concerned

PASSAGE 89:

We have set ourselves a very stiff task but it is by no means beyond our
ability to make a success of this appeal.   Our target is six thousand
pounds and we hope to reach that figure in about one year from now.   In
fact, although I have said it will be a hard task to collect such a huge
sum in so short a time, it could well be that six thousand pounds is a
conservative estimate of the amount we shall need to help these children,
so perhaps we had better regard this as our first target.   However, I
acknowledge that six thousand pounds will give us, at the very least, a
nice start.   Our first event will be next week's 'bring and buy' sale.
We already have over a hundred articles of clothing and goodness knows
what people will bring on the day of the sale.   Our second event will
take place during the following week, when two of our younger members will
attack the world record for playing table tennis.   I am not quite sure
what that means, but I believe they will be playing the game non-stop
for something like twenty-four hours and expect to raise several hundred
pounds while doing so.   I wish them well, and hope their devotion to our
cause does not result in disaster.   In addition to these and other special
events we shall be holding regular raffles throughout the year and I imagine

these will provide us with²⁵⁰ our chief source of income. As far as I am²⁶⁰ concerned, the highlight of the year will be the special²⁷⁰ exhibition of paintings and pottery which we intend to put²⁸⁰ on on Midsummer's Day. As you know, a special committee²⁹⁰ has been formed to organise this exhibition and I am³⁰⁰ pleased to tell you they have managed to book the³¹⁰ Memorial Hall for this event, so there should be plenty³²⁰ of room for all the exhibits. Finally, ladies and gentlemen,³³⁰ I must mention the Sports Day which is planned to³⁴⁰ take place in August. The children themselves will be the³⁵⁰ only competitors and I am sure the whole village will³⁶⁰ turn out to cheer them on. I hope that day³⁷⁰ in particular, will be blessed with good weather. August can³⁸⁰ be one of the wettest as well as one of³⁹⁰ the warmest months. Let us hope for the best.   399 words

FACILITY DRILL 90:

⌐ꟼ Madam Chairman (<u>Note</u>: ꟼ Mr. Chairman)	Ụₒ your Worships	
₹ all the evidence	ઠ bearing in mind	or ⅃ infer
₹ₑc innocence	ⁿℓ unusual ₹ alibi	⅃ᶅ in question
6ₐ bedsitter	⨍⨍ fateful 6₌ substantiate	

PASSAGE 90:

Madam Chairman, Your Worships, Having heard all the evidence in¹⁰ this case, and bearing in mind that my client is²⁰ well known to the court, I find my task an³⁰ exceedingly difficult one. In saying that, I do not wish⁴⁰ you to infer that my belief in my client's innocence⁵⁰ is less than absolute. Whatever he may have done in⁶⁰ the past, there is no doubt in my mind that⁷⁰ he is not guilty of this crime, but I find⁸⁰ myself in the unusal position of having to prove his⁹⁰ innocence rather than merely casting doubts on the case presented¹⁰⁰ by the prosecution. Unhappily, my client is unable to produce¹¹⁰ an alibi for the evening in question. He has told¹²⁰ us how he spent the entire evening alone in his¹³⁰ bedsitter, reading and listening to the radio. When asked to¹⁴⁰ name the programmes he had listened to, he was unable¹⁵⁰ to do so, but I wonder how many people in¹⁶⁰ this court today would be able to recall programmes they¹⁷⁰ had heard on the radio on a particular evening seven 180/ weeks ago.   In any event, it is my client's bad 190/ luck that he can find nobody to substantiate his story 200/ so, as I have said, it is my unusual task 210/ to establish the innocence of a man with no acceptable 220/ alibi. I shall now perform that task by going over 230/ the events of that fateful evening once again and proving 240/ beyond any reasonable doubt that, even if my client had 250/ been at the scene of the crime, he could not 260/ have committed it.   I shall demonstrate that this crime was 270/ committeed by a right-handed person.   My client is left- 280/ handed.   <u>281 words</u>

FACILITY DRILL 91:

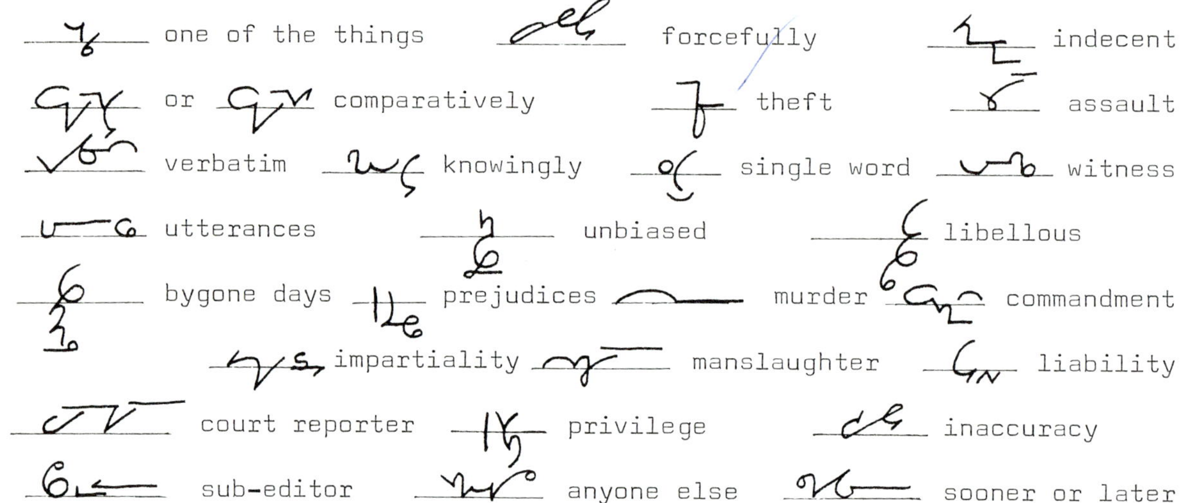

PASSAGE 91:

Recently, I was looking through some back numbers of the 10/ newspaper I work for and one of the things which 20/ struck me most forcefully was the very detailed coverage of 30/ court cases.   In one comparatively minor case of the theft 40/ of a grandfather clock, there was column after column of 50/ verbatim reporting. It seemed that every single word spoken by 60/ every witness had been faithfully taken down in shorthand, transcribed 70/ and printed, and the same applied to the utterances of 80/ judge, counsel and accused.   Today, of course, we are much 90/ more selective both in court and when writing our copy. 100/ Nevertheless, our reports are still governed by the rules of 110/ unbiased reporting which operated in those bygone days.   We have 120/ to write a balanced story and we have to ensure 130/ that our prejudices and opinions as to the guilt or 140/ otherwise of the accused do not find their way into 150/ what we write.   This is not always easy, for the [160] journalist is as human as the next person and anyone [170] who closely follows a murder trial, for example, will soon [180] find himself forming an opinion about the guilt or innocence [190] of the defendent. Even so, impartiality must be the first [200] commandment for the court reporter. The second commandment is accuracy [210] and it is no less important than the first. While [220] an impartial report gives the accused every chance of having [230] a fair trial, an accurate report ensures that the reporter's [240] paper will not find itself on the wrong end of [250] an action for libel. The privilege which gives newspapers protection [260] against libel can be destroyed by inaccuracy. Even a single [270] wrong word can have disastrous consequences: a charge of manslaughter [280] reported as one of murder, or indecent assault as rape. [290] Although there are occasions when a newspaper will decide to [300] take the risk of knowingly publishing something which might be [310] libellous, most libel actions arise from careless errors. These may [320] be due to a lapse of concentration on the part [330] of a reporter when taking or transcribing a shorthand note, [340] or when typing his copy. It is no good blaming [350] the sub-editor or anyone else for failing to spot [360] an error before it gets into print: the responsibility for [370] the accuracy of a story must rest fairly and squarely [380] on the shoulders of the author of that story. The [390] journalist who does not accept that responsibility will, sooner or [400] later, prove to be an expensive liability to his paper. [410]

<u>410 words</u>

<u>FACILITY DRILL 92</u>:

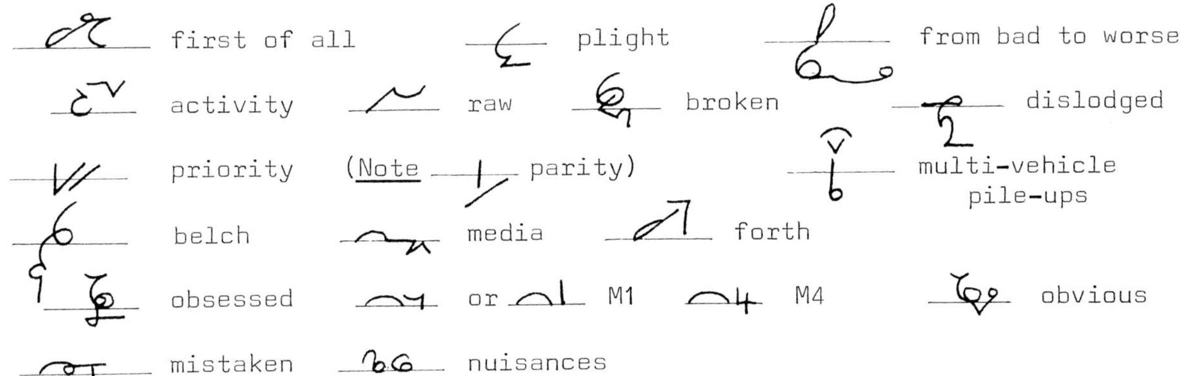

	first of all		plight		from bad to worse
	activity		raw		broken		dislodged
	priority	(<u>Note</u>	parity)		multi-vehicle pile-ups
	belch		media		forth
	obsessed	or	M1	M4		obvious
	mistaken		nuisances

<u>PASSAGE 92</u>:

First of all, I must say how very pleased I [10] am to be here tonight and to have this chance [20] of talking to you about the plight in which today's [30] pedestrians find themselves. Within living memory, ladies and gentlemen, walking 40/ the streets of this town was a safe and pleasant 50/ activity. People walked about the town, not merely to do 60/ their shopping, but because they actually enjoyed being able to 70/ move around in the fresh air. It was not uncommon 80/ for whole families to spend an afternoon in this way, 90/ strolling around the town simply because it was a pleasant 100/ thing to do. What a different picture we have today, 110/ and it is going from bad to worse. Let me 120/ give you a few examples of how the pedestrian is 130/ getting a raw deal nowadays. Consider the pavements first. Why 140/ is it that when paving stones get broken or become 150/ dislodged no-one comes along to repair the damage, but as 160/ soon as a small pothole appears in a road, the 170/ council sends a fleet of lorries and a dozen men 180/ who spend the whole day filling it in? The answer, 190/ ladies and gentlemen, has nothing to do with preventing accidents. 200/ It is all about the powerful lobby which motorists are 210/ able to mount in these days. Only last week I 220/ had to help a blind lady, not to cross the 230/ road, but to cross a section of pavement which presented 240/ more hazards than an army assault course. And what about 250/ the habit which motorists seem to have acquired of parking 260/ on pavements? I should have thought there was a law 270/ against that, but if there is drivers either do not 280/ know about it or do not care.

Narrow pavements are 290/ yet another hazard for the pedestrian, and once again we 300/ must blame the priority given to road users. In these 310/ days, we hear a lot about multi-vehicle pile-ups 320/ on the M1 or M4, but what about 330/ the multi-pedestrian pile-ups in the town centre? Well, 340/ we do not hear about them because the media have 350/ become so obsessed with motoring matters that they have no 360/ time for people who prefer to move about under their 370/ own steam. Finally, I must mention the obvious annoyance and 380/ danger caused by traffic noise and exhaust fumes. Again, I 390/ was under the impression that laws had been passed to 400/ deal with these nuisances, but perhaps I am mistaken. Maybe 410/ the police have more urgent matters to attend to than 420/ chasing noisy vehicles which belch forth great clouds of poisonous 430/ gas.

<u>431 words</u>

<u>End of Section 3</u>

SECTION 4 : Examination Material

<u>INTRODUCTION</u>:

The word 'examinations' usually triggers off a negative response in any
student. In some, the feeling is merely one of apprehension: in others,
sheer terror! In fact, if the necessary preparation has been done, an
examination should be regarded simply as a milestone on the road to a
set goal.

Necessary preparation includes:-

1. Getting plenty of practice in taking dictation for the required length
    of time at the required speed. This builds the writer's confidence,
    and the chances of success are considerably enhanced.

2. Getting some practice in taking dictation at a higher speed than that
    which is required for the examination, but for short periods. This
    helps the writer to cope if the dictation contains sections which
    'read' faster than the rest, possibly because they contain long or
    unfamiliar words.

3. Getting some practice in taking down for longer periods of time than
    required for the examination, i.e. for five or six minutes if the
    examination passage lasts for only three or four.

4. Getting plenty of practice in transcribing pieces of the required
    length in the time which will be allowed.

5. Getting plenty of practice in checking and correcting transcripts.

All this should be achieved well before the examination date arrives.
Unlike the student of academic subjects, the shorthand writer gains nothing
from last-minute 'cramming'.

It is also important that candidates enter the examination room feeling fit
and alert, because fatigue or illness can seriously affect performance.
The whole examination hinges upon a writer's ability to do well in the first
few minutes. If dictation is not successfully taken, then the transcript
will be inaccurate or incomplete.

Finally, remember that work which is badly written and which contains many
spelling errors will not give the examiner a good impression of the writer's
ability and may make the difference between a pass mark or failure in the
case of a borderline candidate.

The following passages have all been used previously for examination purposes and have been arranged in speed order. Although they have been marked in tens to allow them to be read at any speed, the original speeds are shown in brackets, e.g. 2 x 50 (that is, two minutes at 50 w.p.m.), 3 x 50, 2 x 60 and so on.

FACILITY DRILL FOR EXAMINATION PASSAGE 1:

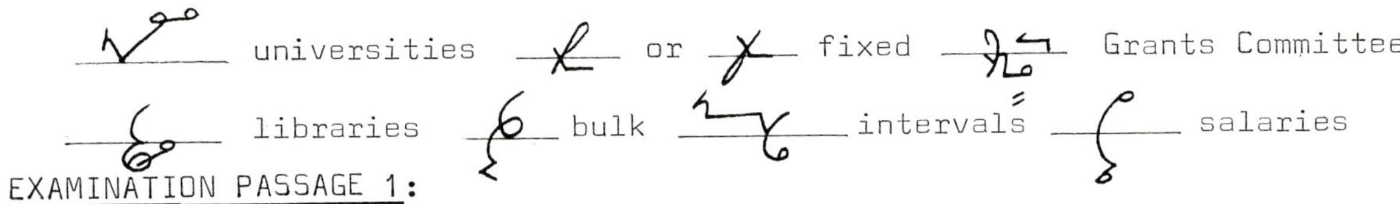

EXAMINATION PASSAGE 1:

<u>Rising Costs at Universities</u> (2 x 50)

Rising costs are causing financial difficulties for many British Universities.[10] This is largely because the bulk of their income is [20] fixed at five-yearly intervals by the University Grants Committee [30] and, although supplementary grants are available, they often come too [40] late to be of real use.   A rise in staff [50] salaries could mean many extra thousands of pounds having to [60] be found in one year. Another difficulty is in knowing [70] how much can be allowed for new buildings which, in [80] turn, affects the numbers of students who can be accepted, [90] and libraries cannot provide sufficient books to satisfy student needs.[100]

100 words

FACILITY DRILL FOR EXAMINATION PASSAGE 2:

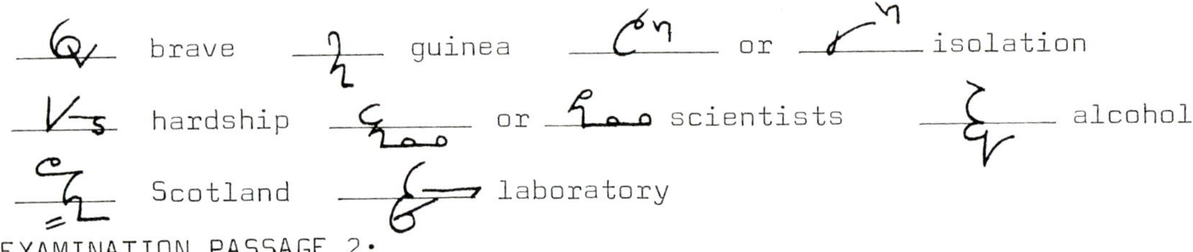

EXAMINATION PASSAGE 2:

<u>Money-Spinners</u> (2 x 50)

There are some strange ways of making money for those [10] brave enough to try them. One is to volunteer to [20] be a guinea pig at the Research Centre for the [30] Common Cold.   This involves a certain amount of experimental treatment[4] and patients cannot mix with one another, but if isolation [50] is no hardship, a volunteer can have a week's free [60] holiday with pay. In Scotland, there is a sleep laboratory, /10 where healthy persons who guarantee not to take drugs or /80 alcohol are paid so much a night to have their /90 sleeping movements watched and recorded for the benefit of scientists. /100   100 words

FACILITY DRILL FOR EXAMINATION PASSAGE 3:

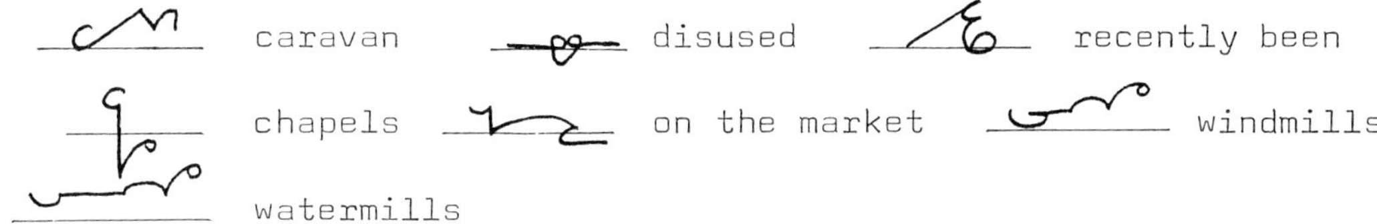

EXAMINATION PASSAGE 3:

Dwelling Places (2 × 50)

Most of us are content to live in an ordinary /10 house, though not everyone is lucky enough to own one /20 and many people have to make do with a flat. /30 For others a caravan provides the answer to the accommodation /40 problem, provided they can find a suitable site on which /50 to keep it. It must be strange, however, to make /70 a home in a disused railway station or a church. /70 Several churches have recently been on the market, as well /80 as chapels, watermills and windmills. The latter have several floors /90 and would, no doubt, be ideal for a large family. /100   100 words

FACILITY DRILL FOR EXAMINATION PASSAGE 4:

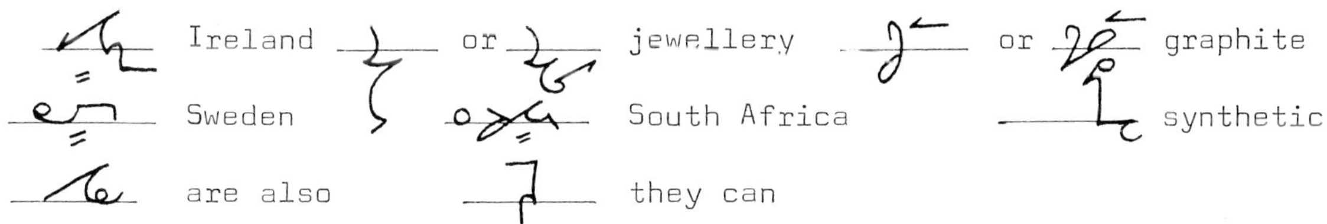

EXAMINATION PASSAGE 4:

Diamonds (2 × 50)

Diamonds are natural stones which must be properly cut before /10 they can be used in jewellery. They can, however, be /20 manufactured from graphite. Apart from being used for ornament, diamonds /30 are also important to industry, as they are needed in /40 cutting,and grinding tools. Synthetic diamonds are produced in Ireland, /50 Sweden and South Africa. There are not enough natural stones /60 to meet industrial demand. It is estimated that

about twelve $\frac{70}{}$ tons a year are required.   Naturally, industrial diamonds
are not $\frac{80}{}$ so expensive as those used in jewellery, but they are $\frac{90}{}$ just as
valuable.   Industry could not easily do without them. $\frac{100}{}$ 100 words

FACILITY DRILL FOR EXAMINATION PASSAGE 5:

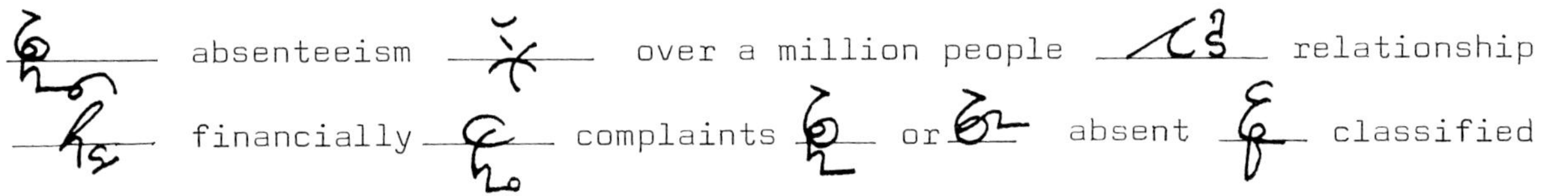

    had things   or   ice-cream   repetitive

     or   muffins   tinny (note: or   = tiny)

     Hot Cross Buns

EXAMINATION PASSAGE 5:

Street Cries (2 x 50)

In olden times, before there were many shops, people who $\frac{10}{}$ had things to sell
would carry their goods through the $\frac{20}{}$ streets calling out what was for sale.
Even when I $\frac{30}{}$ was a child, I can remember hearing the cry 'Hot $\frac{40}{}$ Cross Buns'
on a Good Friday, when men carried trays $\frac{50}{}$ of them through the streets.
Sometimes, on winter days, they $\frac{60}{}$ brought muffins ready for teatime.   The
only cries which are $\frac{70}{}$ heard now seem to be those of the paper sellers $\frac{80}{}$ in
towns.   Unfortunately the tinny and repetitive chimes of ice-$\frac{90}{}$cream vans
seem to have replaced the old street cries. $\frac{100}{}$ 100 words

FACILITY DRILL FOR EXAMINATION PASSAGE 6:

     absenteeism   over a million people   relationship

     financially   complaints   or   absent   classified

EXAMINATION PASSAGE 6:

Absenteeism (2 x 60)

According to a recent report, on any working day, over $\frac{10}{}$ a million people will
be absent from their jobs without $\frac{20}{}$ leave.   One of the main reasons for this
is the $\frac{30}{}$ ease with which they can obtain sickness benefit.   Often they $\frac{40}{}$ stay
away with minor complaints which, while stopping them from $\frac{50}{}$ going to work,
are not enough to cause them to $\frac{60}{}$ stay in bed, or which could really be
classified as $\frac{70}{}$ illnesses.   Some lower-paid workers find they are actually
better $\frac{80}{}$ off financially by taking a few days off sick, but $\frac{90}{}$ the main cause
seems to be a lack of interest $\frac{100}{}$ in the work being done.   Where there is a

good[110]relationship between the employer and the workers, absenteeism is
less.[120]   <u>120 words</u>

<u>FACILITY DRILL FOR EXAMINATION PASSAGE 7:</u>

_____✗_____ or __✗o__ accidents _________ outlay _________ county council

_________ cyclists

<u>EXAMINATION PASSAGE 7:</u>

<u>Road Safety Training</u> (2 × 60)

Research into road accidents reveals that children between four [10]and seven
run the greatest risk, and that boys have twice [20]as many accidents as girls.
In an effort to cut [30]down the number of children involved in road accidents,
one [40]local police force has come up with the idea of [50]installing closed-
circuit television to film children going to school.[60]   The film can then
be shown to the pupils and [70]the police can point out where they are going
wrong.[80]   This could cost the local county council about five hundred [90]
pounds, but if it saved lives, it would be worth[100]the outlay. Police already
visit schools to give road safety[110]talks and show films as well as training
young cyclists.[120]   <u>120 words</u>

<u>FACILITY DRILL FOR EXAMINATION PASSAGE 8:</u>

_________ cultivated _____ or _____ specimen _________ Hampton Court Palace

_________ or _____ flavour _________ or _____ grocer's

<u>EXAMINATION PASSAGE 8:</u>

<u>Herbs</u> (2 × 60)

At one time, it was usual for a herb garden [10] to be cultivated. There is a
fine specimen of such [20] a garden at Hampton Court Palace, which is a
delight [30] to walk through, because the scent given off by many [40] herbs makes
them attractive as plants in themselves and not [50] because they are going to
add flavour to the food [60] we eat. Not many people grow their own herbs
today,[70]as they can be bought ready to use at the [80] grocer's and this saves
a lot of trouble in drying [90] them, which is necessary if they are to be
stored.[100]   Fresh mint, however, always seems to have more flavour than [110]the
dried variety and most gardens manage to produce this.[120]   <u>120 words</u>

FACILITY DRILL FOR EXAMINATION PASSAGE 9:

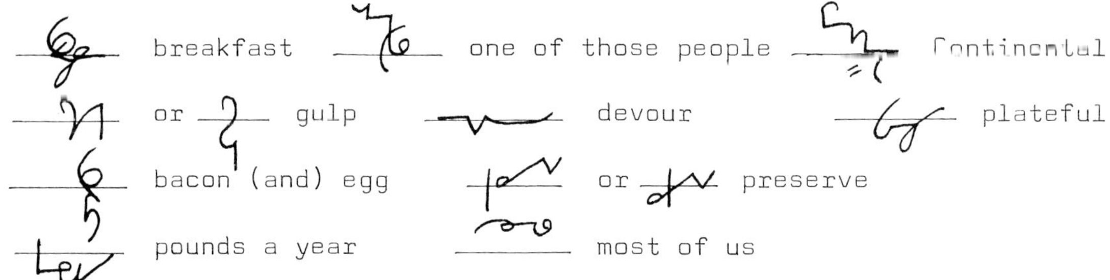

EXAMINATION PASSAGE 9:

Breakfasts (2 × 60)

What do you have for breakfast?   Are you one of [10] those people who rush out of the house still chewing [20] your toast and taking a last gulp of tea? Or [30] do you rise early enough to devour a plateful of [40] bacon and egg in the traditional British way? Perhaps you [50] prefer a Continental breakfast of roll, preserve and coffee, or [60] a Health Food start to the day with fruit and [70] milk.   From a recent report, it would seem that most [80] British people have some kind of cereal, because about fifty [90] million pounds a year is spent on them and four [100] million pounds is spent by the manufacturers in advertising them. [110]   Some people, however, do not eat any breakfast at all. [120]   120 words

FACILITY DRILL FOR EXAMINATION PASSAGE 10:

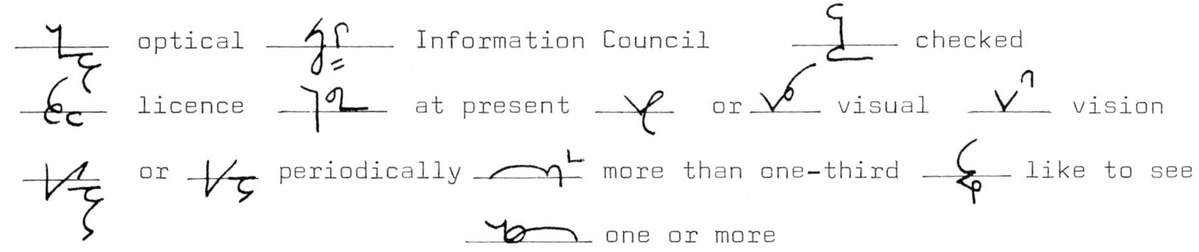

EXAMINATION PASSAGE 10:

Poor Eyesight in Motorists (2 × 70)

In a recently completed survey on more than twenty-two [10] thousand driving licence holders, more than one-third failed to [20] pass one or more of the visual tests, and over [30] four hundred were unable to read a number plate in [40] daylight at twenty-five yards.   The most worrying factor to [50] emerge was that most drivers did not seem to be [60] aware of any defect in their vision.   The Optical Information [70] Council would like to see an eye test a compulsory [80] part of the driving test in future. This would at [90] least weed out those people who are colour-blind.   At [100] present, there is apparently nothing to stop a man who [110] cannot tell the difference between red and green traffic lights [120] from applying for a licence and getting it. In their [130] own interests, all drivers should periodically have their eyesight checked. [140]

140 words

FACILITY DRILL FOR EXAMINATION PASSAGE 11:

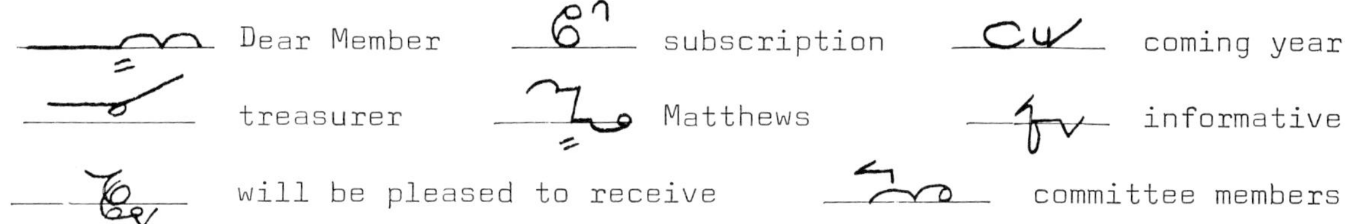

Dear Member	subscription	coming year
treasurer	Matthews	informative
will be pleased to receive		committee members

EXAMINATION PASSAGE 11:

Letter (2 × 70)

Dear Member, This letter is a reminder that your subscription [10] for the coming year is now due. The treasurer will [20] be pleased to receive your cheque and to welcome any [30] new members. Our next meeting will be at Littleton College [40] of Further Education on Saturday, 22nd April, when the speaker [50] will be Mr. Matthews.

We look forward to seeing you [60] and any guests you care to bring, as we are [70] sure this will be a most informative talk.   The enclosed [80] map will help you to find your way to the [90] College. Please complete and return the attached slip if you [100] would like to have tea after the meeting, so that [110] we can make the necessary arrangements. Will committee members please [120] note that there will be a short meeting at two [130] thirty, prior to the talk at three p.m.   Yours sincerely. [140]

140 words

FACILITY DRILL FOR EXAMINATION PASSAGE 12:

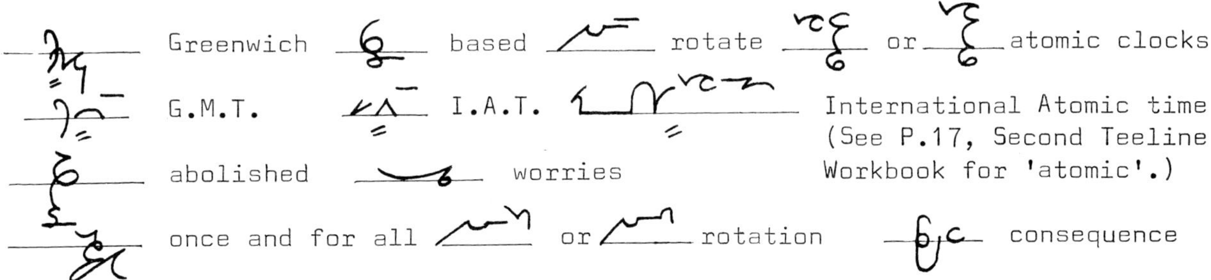

Greenwich	based	rotate	or atomic clocks
G.M.T.	I.A.T.	International Atomic time (See P.17, Second Teeline Workbook for 'atomic'.)	
abolished	worries		
once and for all	or rotation	consequence	

EXAMINATION PASSAGE 12:

Time (2 × 70)

Most people know that Greenwich Moun Time is what we set our clocks by. This is based on the time it takes the earth to rotate in relation to fixed stars.   Now it has been discovered that atomic clocks keep a much more accurate time record, and from this year, G.M.T. will be replaced by I.A.T., that is, International Atomic Time.   Atomic time has been recorded since nineteen-fifty-eight using a master atomic clock in Paris. As the movement of the earth varies, time measured in relation to the earth's rotation also varies a few seconds. This is of little consequence to the majority of us, but worries the scientists. I wish they would worry enough about British Summer Time to get the silly business of putting our clocks backwards and forwards an hour abolished once and for all.

140 words

FACILITY DRILL FOR EXAMINATION PASSAGE 13:

EXAMINATION PASSAGE 13:

Regular Car Maintenance (3 × 50)

Am I getting the best out of my car? This is a question which every car owner should ask himself at least once a year.   Many people have to save for a long time, or else borrow a lot of money, in order to buy a car, and yet they do not seem to think it is worthwhile to look after it properly. Of course, major repairs have to be carried out by experts, but regular maintenance can be done by the average man or woman who has very little technical knowledge.   There are several books on the market which explain in simple terms how to do those little jobs which will help to prolong the life of the engine, ensure trouble-free starting and achieve an economical level of fuel consumption. Also, it is worth bearing in mind that a well-maintained car is nearly always a safe car.

150 words

FACILITY DRILL FOR EXAMINATION PASSAGE 14:

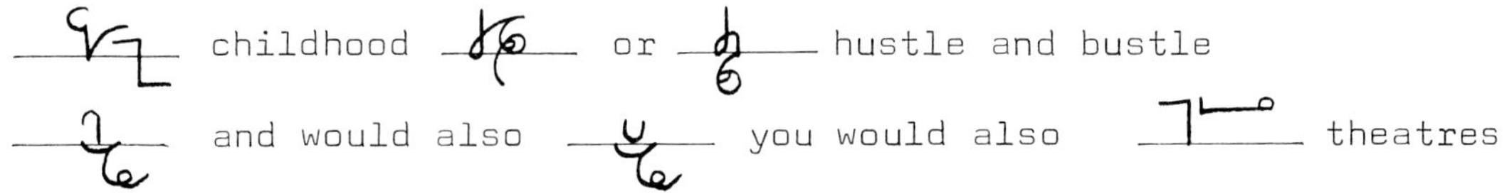

EXAMINATION PASSAGE 14:

Comparing Town and Country Life (3 × 50)

Would you rather live in a large town or in a small country village?
The answer you give to that question will probably depend on where you
spent the early years of your life. If your childhood was spent in a
town, you will have become accustomed to the hustle and bustle of town
life and would probably find life in a village much too quiet and slow-
moving. You would also miss the places of entertainment, such as
cinemas and theatres, and the large shops and stores with their wide
range of goods. On the other hand, if you grew up in the country, you
will have learned to appreciate the benefits of living close to nature
and you would probably find life in a town or city far too noisy and
fast-moving. Certainly, it must be more healthy to live in the country
than in a large town.   150 words

FACILITY DRILL FOR EXAMINATION PASSAGE 15:

EXAMINATION PASSAGE 15

Arranging an A.G.M. (3 × 50)

Dear Bill, As you know, the Annual General Meeting of the Association is
due to be held in October, and I would appreciate your assistance in
deciding upon both the date and venue.   At the meeting of the Executive
Committee in April, there seemed to be a general feeling that this year
we should depart from our usual practice of hiring a hall in Richmond and
try to book a large room at some hotel in Nelson. I should like to
know what you think of that idea and, since you live in Nelson, whether
or not you know of a suitable place.   As far as the date is concerned,
I think either the first or second Saturday in October would be best, but

I would not rule out either [130] of the other two Saturdays. I look forward to hearing [140] from you in the very near future. Best regards, Simon. [150]

150 words

FACILITY DRILL FOR EXAMINATION PASSAGE 16:

birth   or   bonds   or   final decision

possible moment   witnessed   or   childbirth

EXAMINATION PASSAGE 16:

<u>Father and Child</u> (3 x 60)

In many countries it is now the accepted thing for [10] a father to be present at the birth of his [20] child.   It is believed that this helps to strengthen the [30] bonds between the mother, the father and the baby. This [40] trend towards involving the father with his child from the [50] earliest possible moment has much to recommend it, but it [60] is not something which should be forced on the father. [70] There are still many men who regard childbirth as an [80] occasion for women only, and such men are probably best [90] kept well away from the scene.   There are also, of [100] course, a lot of women who do not want their [110] husbands to be present at the birth and it is [120] surely right that the final decision on the matter should [130] be made by the mother. Certainly, most fathers who are [140] present when their wives give birth seem to find it [150] a wonderful experience. A friend of mine has witnessed the [160] birth of every one of his three children and he [170] is now looking forward to seeing the fourth child born. [180]

180 words

FACILITY DRILL FOR EXAMINATION PASSAGE 17:

Minister of Agriculture   Annual Conference   up to now

National Association (See Page 18, Second Teeline Workbook)

or   . protein   Government's polic

Government's view   members of the Association

or   alternative   agricultural industry

alert   world-wide   or   farmers

EXAMINATION PASSAGE 17:

Nut Farming (3 x 60)

The Minister of Agriculture spoke yesterday to the Annual Conference /10 of the National Association of Farmers about the Government's policy /20 of encouraging farmers to use part of their land for /30 the production of nuts. He said that there would have /40 to be radical changes in farming techniques over the next /50 few years in order to meet the rising world-wide demand /60 for protein. Up to now, farmers had tried to satisfy /70 this demand by increasing their herds of livestock, but said /80 the Minister, a nut crop would give a far higher /90 yield of protein per acre. The Government was in the /100 process of working out a scheme to give financial help /110 to farmers who planted nut trees. This scheme would include /120 a guarantee against crop failure during the first five years /130 of production. The Minister ended his speech by urging members /140 of the Association to be always alert to the possibilities /150 of growing alternative crops, particularly those which were not usually /160 grown in this country. In the Government's view, this was /170 the best way to bring about a prosperous agricultural industry. /180 180 words

FACILITY DRILL FOR EXAMINATION PASSAGE 18:

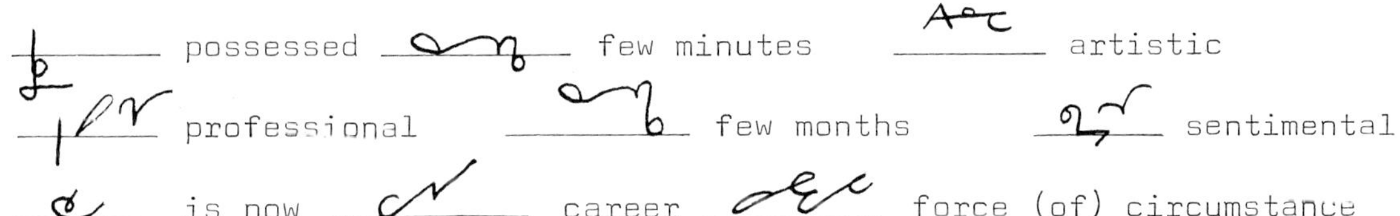

	possessed		few minutes		artistic
	professional		few months		sentimental
	is now		career		force (of) circumstance

EXAMINATION PASSAGE 18:

Artistic Talent (3 x 60)

Many years ago, when I was still at school, I /10 had a friend who possessed a wonderful gift for drawing /20 and painting. While it took me a long time to /30 produce a picture which looked anything like the object I /40 was supposed to be drawing, he would produce a far /50 better picture in a matter of a few minutes. He /60 was not particularly good at any other subject, but his /70 artistic skill made him one of the most popular boys /80 in the school, and everyone was convinced that when he /90 left school he would become a professional artist. A few /100 months ago, I made a sentimental journey back to my /110 old school, where I enquired if anyone knew what had /120 happened to my old friend. You can imagine my surprise[130] upon being told that he is now the manager of[140] a bank in Sydney, Australia. I wonder if he chose[150] a career in banking or if he found himself in[160] it by force of circumstance. Perhaps he still exercises his[170] talent for art in his spare time. I hope so.[180]

180 words

FACILITY DRILL FOR EXAMINATION PASSAGE 19:

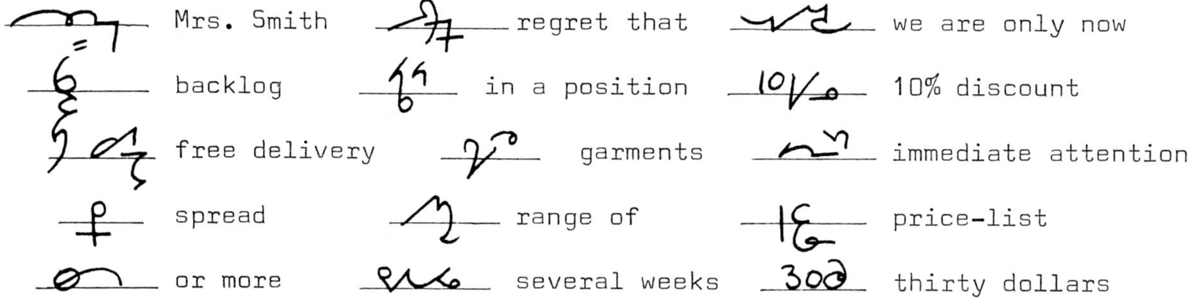

	Mrs. Smith		regret that		we are only now
	backlog		in a position		10% discount
	free delivery		garments		immediate attention
	spread		range of		price-list
	or more		several weeks		thirty dollars

EXAMINATION PASSAGE 19:

<u>Baby Clothes</u> (3 × 60)

Dear Mrs. Smith, Thank you for your enquiry about our[10] baby clothes. We regret that we have been such a[20] long time in answering your letter, but our factory has[30] been closed for repairs during the past two weeks, and[40] we are only now beginning to catch up on the[50] backlog of work. The fire which damaged the factory building[60] spread to our nearby warehouse and destroyed twenty per cent[70] of our stock of baby clothes, and it will be[80] several weeks before we are in a position to give[90] immediate attention to all our customers' orders. However, we are[100] enclosing our amended catalogue from which you will see that[110] we produce a very wide range of garments to fit[120] babies of all ages up to three years. You will[130] note from the price-list that we offer a ten[140] per cent discount and free delivery service on all orders[150] to the value of thirty dollars or more. We trust[160] you will be able to find something to suit you[170] and look forward to receiving your order shortly. Yours faithfully.[180]

180 words

FACILITY DRILL FOR EXAMINATION PASSAGE 20:

							route
	have their own		magnificent		scenery		brochure

<u>EXAMINATION PASSAGE 20</u>:

<u>Advertising Circular</u> (2 x 80)

Dear Sir or Madam, How would you like to tour /Scotland by car and leave the worry of the hotel /booking to us?   We will send you a free map / showing you the most interesting route to take, and we /will also suggest the best hotels for you to stay /in. Every hotel on your chosen route will welcome you /in the evening with a variety of choice food and / excellent entertainment. Several have their own heated swimming pools. You /can opt for superb luxury, or for an economy holiday./ In either case, the service will be to your satisfaction./ In addition to the magnificent scenery, fishing, golf and tennis /can be arranged. Your tour can be planned for any /length of time and there are special rates for children./ <u>You</u> decide what kind of holiday you want and <u>we</u>/will make all the reservations for you. Write for our /free brochure and start planning your holiday now. Yours faithfully./   <u>160 words</u>

<u>FACILITY DRILL FOR EXAMINATION PASSAGE 21</u>:

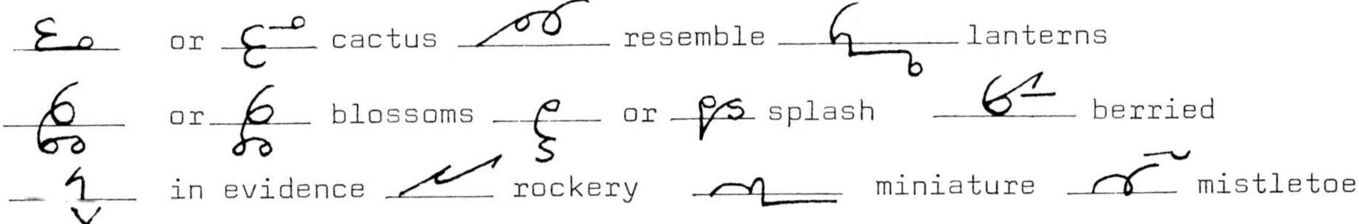

<u>EXAMINATION PASSAGE 21</u>:

<u>Christmas Plants</u> (2 x 80)

This year, I had a Christmas cactus as a present./ It has pink flowers which, when open, resemble Chinese lanterns./ Some plants carry dozens of blossoms at once, and make /a lovely splash of colour. Small berried plants in pots /are also in evidence over the Christmas period, and are / often a better buy than holly.   I am lucky enough /to have two holly bushes in the garden, but they /never bear berries, so each year I mix the leaves /with the small rosy berries which form on my miniature /roses in the rockery.   Some people like to have mistletoe /too, but it is said that a berry should be /removed each time a couple kiss under it, as the /old belief was that each berry carried a blessing which /had to be taken away.

If it is a mild[140] winter, it is often possible to bring in the last[150] of the roses to add colour to any Christmas display.[160]

160 words

FACILITY DRILL FOR EXAMINATION PASSAGE 22:

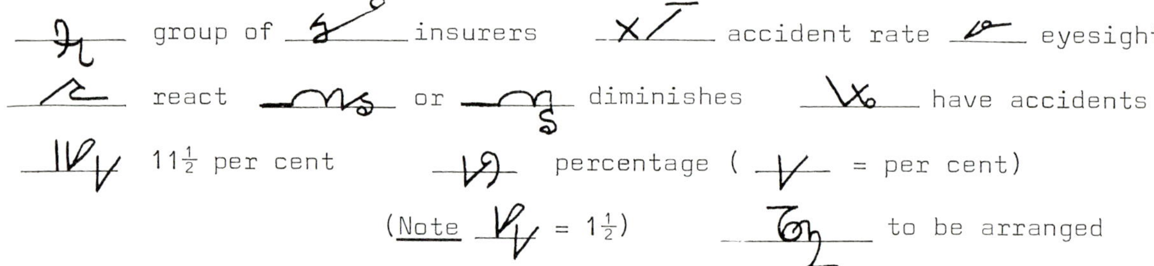

EXAMINATION PASSAGE 22:

Age and Driving (2 × 80)

In a study carried out by a leading group of [10] motor insurers, it was discovered that as a motorist's age [20] rises, his accident rate decreases. A quarter of drivers who [30] are under twenty years of age are involved in some [40] accident during a year, but this percentage diminishes until at [50] seventy years of age, only 11½ per [60] cent have accidents. This is probably because the older drivers [70] are more experienced and have learned not to take risks.[80] Young people do not always see danger in a situation,[90] but only feel the excitement of the moment. However, there [100] are snags in getting older. One's eyesight, for instance, tends[110] to deteriorate and one's general health may also decline, making[120] the driver less alert or causing him to react more [130] slowly in an emergency. Now the scheme which gives people[140] driving licences till they are seventy is operating, regular checks[150] on eyesight and health will doubtless have to be arranged.[160]

160 words

FACILITY DRILL FOR EXAMINTION PASSAGE 23:

EXAMINATION PASSAGE 23:

Take a Bus (2 × 80)

Many experiments are being carried out at the moment to ^{10} see how cars can be prevented from coming into city ^{20} centres. In some places, one-way traffic systems are in ^{30} operation and the traffic is kept out of certain shopping ^{40} areas which are reserved for pedestrians. This has radically changed ^{50} the appearance of many town centres and is sometimes confusing ^{60} to motorists and walkers alike until they get used to ^{70} the new arrangements. In other places, although cars are banned ^{80} from the town centre, buses are allowed to penetrate, so ^{90} that shoppers may be set down and picked up outside ^{100} the shops. The aim of many town councils is to ^{110} ensure a regular bus service within easy walking distance of ^{120} every home, so that it is more convenient to take ^{130} a bus than to find a parking space for the ^{140} car. However, the old and disabled still have a problem ^{150} as they cannot always walk to the nearest bus stop. ^{160} 160 words

FACILITY DRILL FOR EXAMINATION PASSAGE 24:

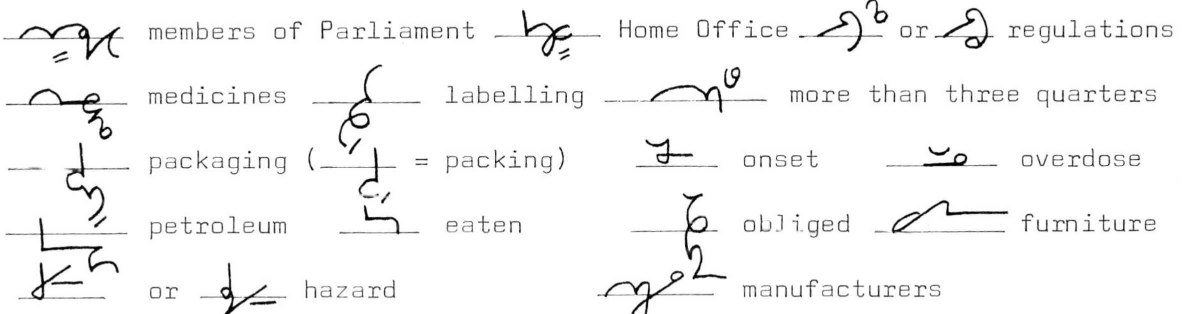

members of Parliament — Home Office — or — regulations

medicines — labelling — more than three quarters

packaging (— = packing) — onset — overdose

petroleum — eaten — obliged — furniture

or — hazard — manufacturers

EXAMINATION PASSAGE 24:

Dangers of Unlabelled Products (2 × 80)

Members of Parliament have been pressing the Home Office to ^{10} introduce regulations to cover the labelling and packaging of a ^{20} wide range of house-hold products which could be dangerous if ^{30} eaten by children. Over seven thousand children are admitted to ^{40} hospital each year, suffering from this kind of poisoning. More ^{50} than three-quarters of them are under five years old ^{60} and, on average, ten a year die. In Canada and ^{70} the United States, manufacturers are obliged to put adequate warnings ^{80} on the package but, in

Britain, similar products can be sold without. Furniture polish, for example, may be petroleum based. Another hazard for children is when medicines are left within reach. Pills and capsules often look like sweets, and a child may take an overdose which could prove fatal, especially if the parents do not discover the reason for a sudden onset of illness in time. Medicines, like matches, should be kept well out of the reach of the young.

160 words

FACILITY DRILL FOR EXAMINATION PASSAGE 25:

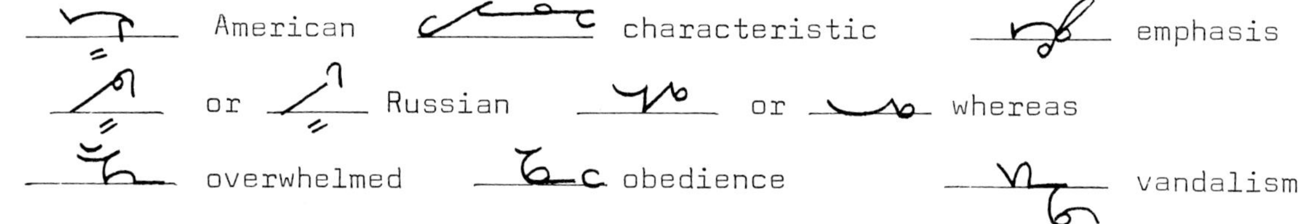

EXAMINATION PASSAGE 25:

Reading and Learning (2 x 90)

An American survey of reading books in thirteen countries reveals some interesting facts. They presented certain sets of values and attitudes which could be considered to be characteristic of the country in which they were used. As might be expected, in English books, emphasis was placed on situations involving games and sports, whereas Russian ones tended to stress the importance of work, rather than play; but in neither country did war, religion or obedience to authority figure in reading books. In most countries the main theme of stories was the various ways in which people get on with each other. In Indian books, much stress was placed on family situations, old people, tradition and religion. If a child learns his attitudes to life generally through his early reading material, then it may be time someone wrote a few new books stressing the importance of not dropping litter, having respect for property and other such matters. Maybe this would be one way to combat the vandalism which appears to be ever increasing, before we are overwhelmed by litter and violence.

180 words

FACILITY DRILL FOR EXAMINATION PASSAGE 26:

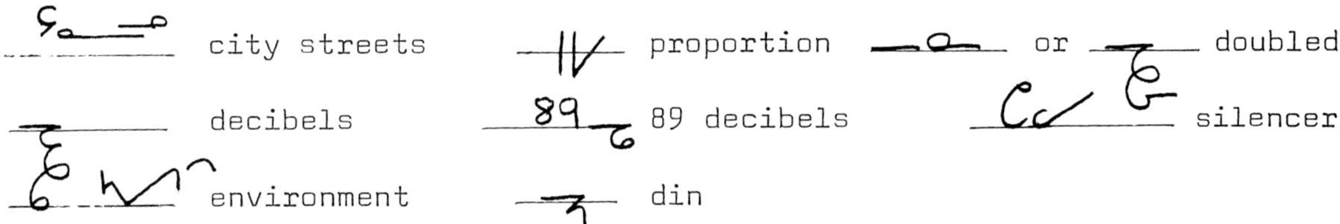

EXAMINATION PASSAGE 26:

Street Noise (2 x 90)

A survey carried out a few years ago in city ^{10} streets to measure noise levels, showed that in nine years ^{20} traffic noise had increased by fifty per cent and that ^{30} lorries and buses were amongst the worst offenders. Noise on ^{40} roads which carried a high proportion of heavy traffic had, ^{50} in some cases, doubled in the past nine years. Noise ^{60} is measured in decibels by meters. The present legal limit ^{70} for the heaviest lorries is 89 decibels, but even this ^{80} allowed far too much noise to be made. One way ^{90} to reduce noise is to make sure the vehicle's silencer ^{100} is operating properly and, as these deteriorate with wear, they ^{110} need regular checking. The odd thing about noise, whether it ^{120} is in the street or the home, is that it ^{130} expands. In a noisy environment a person will have to ^{140} shout to make himself heard, thus adding to the general ^{150} din, and car drivers will have to sound their horns ^{160} louder to give warning of their approach, whereas in a ^{170} quiet room or street, normal sound can be heard easily. ^{180}

<u>180 words</u>

FACILITY DRILL FOR EXAMINATION PASSAGE 27:

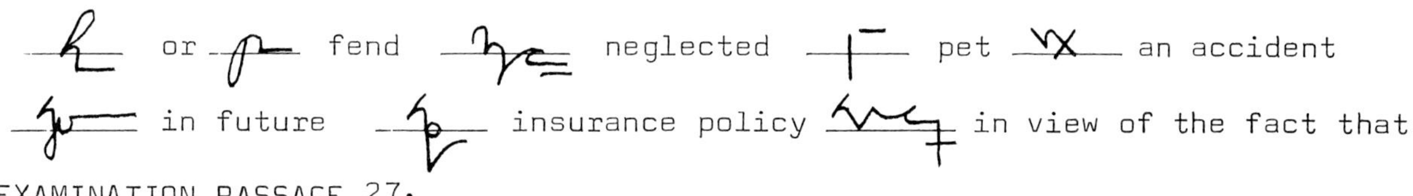

EXAMINATION PASSAGE 27:

The Animals Act (2 x 90)

Owning an animal is a responsibility, although many people who ^{10} buy animals do not seem to realise it. They think ^{20} it will be fun to have a puppy or a ^{30} horse and then find it is a nuisance to have ^{40} to exercise it properly and an expense to give it ^{50} the proper kind of food. Cats, at least, can fend ^{60} for themselves if they are neglected. According to British law, ^{70} if a pet causes an accident or damage, its owner ^{80} could be in serious trouble as he may have to ^{90} foot the bill. This seems reasonable in view of the ^{100} fact that every year straying dogs cause accidents on the ^{110} roads and that sometimes they worry sheep, or even kill ^{120} them, to say nothing of the numbers of postmen they ^{130} bite. In future it will pay an owner to train ^{140} his pet, to keep it under control at all times ^{150} and to take out an insurance policy to cover him ^{160} against possible claims for damages. When these facts become widely ^{170} known, people will probably think twice before buying a pet. ^{180} 180 words

FACILITY DRILL FOR EXAMINATION PASSAGE 28:

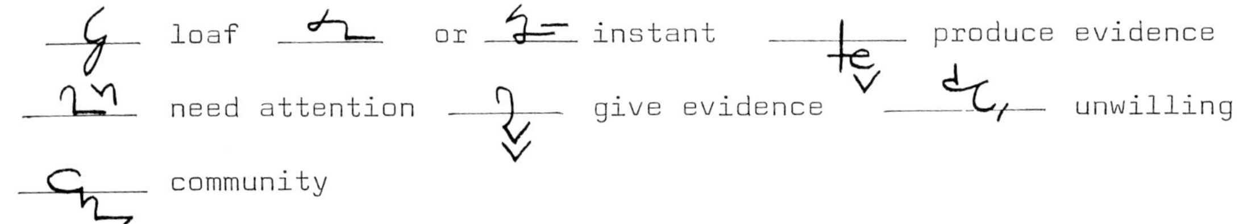

loaf   or   instant   produce evidence

need attention   give evidence   unwilling

community

EXAMINATION PASSAGE 28:

Making Complaints (2 x 90)

What do you do if you buy a loaf of ^{10} wrapped bread and discover on removing the wrapper that it ^{20} is mouldy, or if you find a piece of glass ^{30} in your jar of instant coffee? What you should do ^{40} is to report the matter to your local food inspector. ^{50} However, unless you can produce evidence of where and when ^{60} you purchased the offending article, and unless you are prepared ^{70} to appear in court to give evidence, it is no ^{80} use seeking him out. It is better to approach the ^{90} retailer or manufacturer through official channels, as they are more ^{100} likely to take notice, and it may be that some ^{110} of their methods or machinery need attention. Most firms try ^{120} to put things right by replacing the article, sometimes with ^{130} several in the place of one. After all, they want ^{140} to retain the customer's goodwill. As a nation, the British ^{150} seem to be unwilling to make complaints about bad service ^{160} but, if it is done in a reasonable way, it ^{170} is in the interests of the community to do so. ^{180}

                    180 words

FACILITY DRILL FOR EXAMINATION PASSAGE 29:

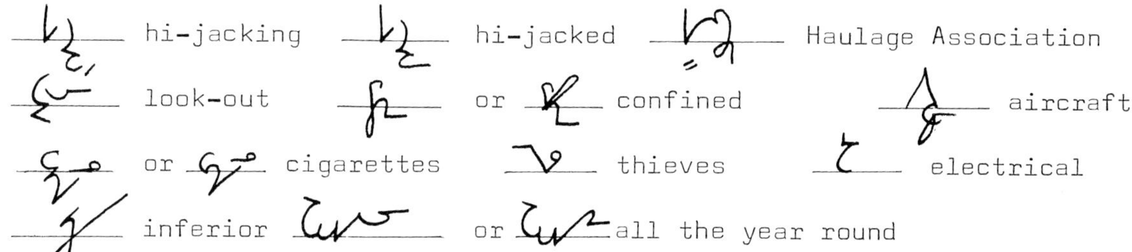

hi-jacking   hi-jacked   Haulage Association

look-out   or   confined   aircraft

or   cigarettes   thieves   electrical

inferior   or   all the year round

EXAMINATION PASSAGE 29:

Lorry Thefts (2 x 100)

Hi-jacking is not confined to aircraft.   Every week, lorries are [10]hi-jacked and may turn up later, minus their loads.   The [20]weeks before Christmas are the busiest, when items such as [30]wines, spirits and cigarettes are popular loads for the thieves.[40]   This kind of crime involves much organisation and is usually [50]done on a large scale, as the goods must be [60]lodged in some kind of warehouse until they can be [70]got rid of.   Clothing and electrical goods are popular all [80]the year round, as there is always a market for [90]them.   They can be sold at well below the normal[100]prices, and people will always buy a cut-price article,[110]even though they may find they have been sold something[120]inferior, or suspect from the price that they are buying[130]stolen goods. The Road Haulage Association has its own network[140]of patrols who keep a look-out for stolen vehicles, and[150]report their findings to the police but, although the number[160]of these crimes has been reduced over the past five[170]years, there are still over three thousand a year, and[180]only a small percentage of the stolen goods is recovered.[190] There seems to be no easy answer to this problem.[200]

200 words

FACILITY DRILL FOR EXAMINATION PASSAGE 30:

safety   as is   antagonistic

EXAMINATION PASSAGE 31:

Seat Belts (2 x 100)

Every time I go out in my car, I try [10]to remember to fasten my safety belt before setting off.[20]   This can be a nuisance if I am getting out [30]at short intervals to do shopping, but research into accidents [40]has shown that wearing a seat belt can halve the ⁵⁰risk of death or serious injury. Many people think they ⁶⁰are not likely to be involved in an accident unless ⁷⁰they are travelling at speed on a motorway, but accidents ⁸⁰can happen to the most careful motorist when he least ⁹⁰expects it and, as the old saying goes, 'It is¹⁰⁰better to be safe than sorry'. The Road Research Laboratory¹¹⁰has been experimenting with other methods of preventing passengers and¹²⁰drivers from being thrown out of the car or injured¹³⁰inside it in the event of a crash, but these¹⁴⁰are all more expensive than seat belts. Another solution is¹⁵⁰to pass a law making it compulsory for seat belts¹⁶⁰to be worn, as is already the case in some¹⁷⁰countries, but there is much opposition to it here. It¹⁸⁰is surprising how many people are antagonistic to measures designed¹⁹⁰for their protection. I am trying hard to be sensible.²⁰⁰   <u>200 words</u>

FACILITY DRILL FOR EXAMINATION PASSAGE 32:

one would have   or   oneself (<u>Note</u>:   yourself)

EXAMINATION PASSAGE 32:

<u>Book Clubs</u> (3 × 70)

For the person who likes reading books there is a ¹⁰lot to be said for being a member of a ²⁰book club. These clubs offer books for sale at prices ³⁰which are considerably below what one would have to pay ⁴⁰for the same books in a shop, and members are ⁵⁰able to make their choice from a list of many ⁶⁰of the latest titles. Many people become members of a ⁷⁰book club by accepting an introductory offer of, for instance, ⁸⁰four books for five pounds and promising to purchase at ⁹⁰least four more books during their first year of membership.¹⁰⁰ Some clubs offer books on a very wide range of¹¹⁰subjects, from gardening to exploring and from fishing to poetry.¹²⁰ Others cater for readers with special interests, such as motoring¹³⁰or ancient history. Membership of a book club is a¹⁴⁰very good way of building up a small private library¹⁵⁰but one should be careful not to commit oneself to¹⁶⁰buying more books than one can afford. I have a¹⁷⁰friend who has been a member of no fewer than¹⁸⁰three book clubs at the same time for about ten¹⁹⁰years. She says buying books has become a habit with²⁰⁰her, although she admits she can no longer afford it./ 210   <u>210 words</u>

FACILITY DRILL FOR EXAMINATION PASSAGE 33 :

_____ photographic   _____ recent letter   _____ formation

_____ in any way   _____ existence   _____ anticipation   (See Second
Teeline Workbook, P.28)

EXAMINATION PASSAGE 33 :

<u>A New Photographic Society</u> (3 × 70)

Dear Mr. Brown, I was interested in your recent letter /[10] to our local
newspaper in which you proposed the formation /[20] of a photographic society
in this town. You invited people /[30] to get in touch with you if they
thought they /[40] would be able to help in any way and I /[50] hope this letter
is the kind of response you are /[60] looking for. Perhaps the first thing I
should mention is /[70] that I have recently retired from work and would,
therefore, /[80] be both able and willing to devote a lot of /[90] time to the
affairs of the society. I think this /[100] would be most important during
the early stages when we /[110] would be trying to drum up support and make
the /[120] existence of the society known throughout the area. There is /[130] also
another way in which I would be able to /[140] help such a body to make a start.
Although I /[150] have never earned my living by photography, I have always /[160]
had a keen interest in the subject and have gathered /[170] together, over the
years, a large collection of photographic equipment. /[180] I should be only too
pleased to place this equipment /[190] at the disposal of the other members
during the early /[200] days of the society. Yours in keen anticipation.
William Roberts. /[210]   <u>210 words</u>

FACILITY DRILL FOR EXAMINATION PASSAGE 34 :

_____ that this Company   _____ Corporation   (<u>Note</u> _____ co-operation)

_____ union   _____ taken over   _____ or   _____ negotiations

_____ redundancies   _____ foreseeable   _____ you will also

EXAMINATION PASSAGE 34:

A Takeover Bid (3 × 70)

Ladies and gentlemen, No doubt, you will all have read /10 the recent reports in the local newspaper which suggest that /20 this company has been the subject of a takeover bid /30 by a large international corporation. You will also have heard /40 the rumours which have been going round the factory. It /50 was because of those rumours that your Board of Directors /60 instructed me to call this special meeting of supervisors and /70 union representatives. What I have to tell you, in fact, /80 is that this firm will shortly be taken over by /90 a much larger company, but not by the international corporation /100 mentioned in those newspaper reports. The negotiations are now /110 in their final stages and it is expected that the deal /120 will be completed within the next few days. This means /130 that, in the very near future, there will be changes /140 in the composition of the Board of Directors, and it /150 is quite possible that these will be followed by changes /160 in the way the firm is run. I have been /170 asked to make it quite clear to you, however, that /180 there will be no redundancies in the foreseeable future. The /190 firm will continue to trade under its present name and /200 its policy of expansion will continue to operate as planned. /210   210 words

FACILITY DRILL FOR EXAMINATION PASSAGE 35:

_____ culprits _____ maintenance _____ it seems to me

EXAMINATION PASSAGE 35:

Fighting Vandalism (3 × 80)

Mr. Chairman, It seems to me that some of the /10 people who have already spoken this evening have no idea /20 of the magnitude of the problem facing the Council. We /30 are not concerned with occasional acts of vandalism, such as /40 those we have met with in the past. We now /50 have to deal, not only with the odd person who /60 throws a brick through a window, but with groups of /70 young people who seem to have nothing better to do /80 than to wander around town every evening, looking for something /90 to damage or destroy. Those people who say this is /100 a matter for the police are quite right, but it /110 is also a big problem for the Council, because repairs /120 to

public property are costing us thousands of pounds each[130] year. It is
estimated that this year we shall have[140] to find an extra two thousand
pounds, over and above[150] our normal maintenance costs, to pay for damaged
street lights[160] and an extra one thousand pounds to replace broken windows[170]
in buildings owned by the Council. The police are doing[180] their best to
catch the culprits but I think we[190] should be doing more to protect
property from acts of[200] vandalism. We could, for example, protect our
street lights by[210] placing wire cages round them. This has been done in[220]
other towns where vandalism is a problem and I am[230] told that it is much
cheaper than repairing broken lights.[240]   240 words

FACILITY DRILL FOR EXAMINATION PASSAGE 36:

_____ threat _____ at this stage _____ premature _____ or _____ hopeful

EXAMINATION PASSAGE 36:

Part of Speech about a threat to close a village school (3 × 80)

Ladies and gentlemen, I am sure you were all as [10] concerned as I was to hear
that our village school [20] is under the threat of closure. It seems that
the [30] building which is now seventy-four years old, can no [40] longer be
regarded as a suitable place in which to [50] educate our children. The main
problem is one of safety.[60] According to the report I have just read, there
is [70] some danger that unless repairs are carried our very soon [80] the entire
roof will collapse. There is also a long [90] and serious crack in one of the
walls.   Now, although[100] I am not an expert on such matters, it seems[110] to
me that to talk about closing the school is,[120] at this stage, rather
premature. There is no suggestion in[130] the report that the building is beyond
repair and I[140] am hopeful that the school can be saved. If[150] it is closed,
our children will have to travel at[160] least eight miles to school each day,
and that will[170] be a great inconvenience both to them and to us.[180] I must also
say I am sure my children's education[190] would suffer as a result of the
disruption caused by[200] having to change schools. Further, I know I am not[210]
alone in believing that in our village we have the[220] best teachers in the
whole country. For all these reasons,[230] I think we should oppose the closure
of the school.[240]   240 words

FACILITY DRILL FOR EXAMINATION PASSAGE 37:

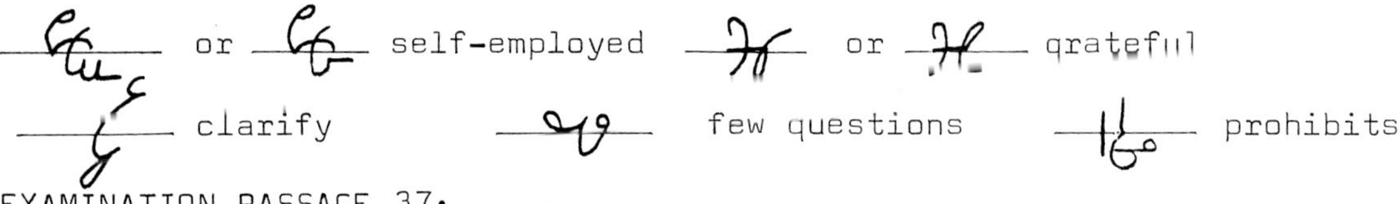

or ________ self-employed ________ or ________ grateful

________ clarify ________ few questions ________ prohibits

EXAMINATION PASSAGE 37:

Letter about a Pension Scheme (3 × 80)

Dear Sirs, I am writing to thank you for the (10) brochure and the additional information on your Pension Scheme for (20) the self-employed. There are, however, one or two points (30) which are by no means clear to me, and I (40) would be most grateful if you could answer a few (50) questions for me. When I made my original enquiry, I (60) made it quite clear that I wished to retire as (70) soon as I reached fifty-five years of age. Unfortunately, (80) all the examples in the brochure are based on a (90) retirement age of either sixty or sixty-five. I wonder (100) if there is a law which prohibits a self-employed (110) person from retiring before sixty years of age?   Perhaps you (120) could clarify the position. My second question is this: What (130) happens if I find that I can no longer afford (140) to pay the premiums? As you are, no doubt, aware, (150) the income of a person who works for himself is (160) likely to vary considerably from year to year and it (170) is often impossible to know what one's financial position will (180) be in a few years' time. Finally, I should like (190) to know if my pension rights would be affected in (200) any way if I decided to live abroad, either before (210) or after my retirement. I am sure you will appreciate (220) the importance of the points I have raised and will (230) favour me with an early reply. Yours faithfully, James Black. (240)   <u>240 words</u>

FACILITY DRILL FOR EXAMINATION PASSAGE 38:

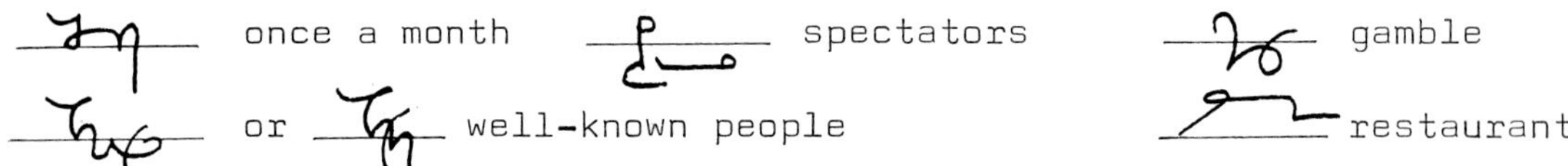

________ once a month ________ spectators ________ gamble

________ or ________ well-known people ________ restaurant

EXAMINATION PASSAGE 38:

A Day at the Races (3 × 90)

If the weather is fine, a day at the races (10) can be a most enjoyable experienc[e]
Even those who do (20) not care to bet on the horses should have no (30) difficulty

in finding something to entertain them. I have a ^{40}friend who goes to race meetings at least once a ^{50}month just for the pleasure of watching the horses as ^{60}they parade before the start of a race. Sometimes she ^{70}takes her camera and comes home with wonderful pictures of ^{80}some of the best racehorses in the country. It is ^{90}quite possible, however, to enjoy yourself at the races even^{100}if you are not fond of horses. Sometimes I get^{110}as much pleasure from watching people in the crowd as^{120}from watching the races. On many occasions, I have seen^{130}well-known people among the spectators, some of them from^{140}the world of entertainment and others from the very different^{150}world of politics. Watching the ordinary spectators can also be^{160}quite amusing. As the horses approach the winning post, some^{170}people shout at the tops of their voices and jump^{180}up and down with excitement. I suppose I would behave^{190}in the same way if I had placed a bet^{200}of several hundred pounds on one of the runners, but^{210}I have never found it necessary to gamble in order^{220}to enjoy myself at the races.

Sometimes, racing takes place^{230}in the evening and, if you are the kind of^{240}person who likes eating out, you can book a table^{250}at the course restaurant and add the pleasure of eating^{260}a good meal to that of watching the horses run.^{270} <u>270 words</u>

<u>FACILITY DRILL FOR EXAMINATION PASSAGE 39</u>:

album   keen   surveys   popularity

personally

<u>EXAMINATION PASSAGE 39</u>:

<u>Stamp Collection</u> (3 x 90)

I may be wrong, but it seems to me that ^{10}stamp collecting is not such a popular hobby today as ^{20}it was when I was a boy. In those days, ^{30}almost every schoolboy had a stamp album and took great ^{40}pride in showing it to anyone who asked to see ^{50}it. It is a strange thing, but I do not ^{60}remember any girls who were keen collectors. However, that may ^{70}be because it was not until I had lost my ^{80}passion for postage stamps that I became interested in what ^{90}girls did in their spare time! Today, we are told,^{100}boys become interested in the opposite sex at a much ^{110} younger age, so perhaps that is one of the reasons ^{120} for the declining popularity of stamp collecting. I have a ^{130} feeling, though, that television has to take a share of ^{140} the blame. The first thing most children do when they ^{150} come home from school is to turn on the television ^{160} and, if we are to believe the latest surveys, they ^{170} are likely to watch it for a total of four ^{180} hours before they go to bed. Personally, I think they ^{190} would be making far better use of their time by ^{200} collecting postage stamps. I would certainly be surprised if anyone ^{210} could tell me of a more educational hobby. Although it ^{220} is not possible for me to say just how much ^{230} it taught me, I am sure that my knowledge of ^{240} history and geography, for instance, would not be so wide-^{250}ranging if I had never been a stamp collector. On ^{260} the other hand I would probably know more about girls. ^{270}

<u>270 words</u>

FACILITY DRILL FOR EXAMINATION PASSAGE 40:

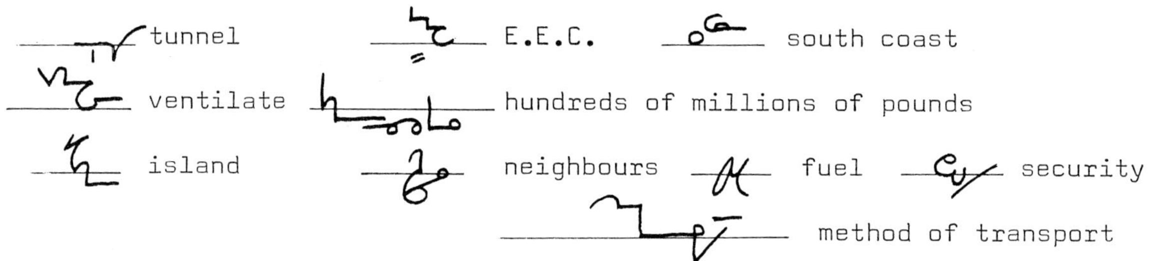

EXAMINATION PASSAGE 40:

<u>A Bridge across the English Channel</u> (3 × 90)

The idea of linking England and France by building either ^{10} a bridge over the English Channel or a tunnel under ^{20} it, is a very old one. At times the arguments ^{30} between those who favour a bridge and those who favour ^{40} a tunnel have been very heated, and this is certainly ^{50} one of the reasons why there has been little practical ^{60} progress. Since Britain joined the E.E.C., the debate ^{70} has taken a new lease of life and it would ^{80} appear that most of the experts support the proposal that ^{90} the south coast of Britain and the north coast of ^{100} France should be connected by a bridge. The chief objection ^{110} to a tunnel is that it would not be possible ^{120} to ventilate it well enough for cars to be driven ^{130} through it and its use would, therefore, have to be ^{140} restricted to trains. On the other hand, it would be ^{150} possible to construct a bridge which could carry both trains[160] and motor vehicles and this would clearly be a far[170] better proposition from the commercial and financial points of view.[180] The bridge, which would be about twenty miles long, would[190] take between five and ten years to build, and would[200] cost hundreds of millions of pounds. However, a lot more[210] talking will have to be done between the French and[220] the British Governments before such a scheme is finally approved[230] and Britain is brought closer than ever to her European[240] neighbours. But, many British people wish to preserve their island[250] security, and with increasing fuel shortages forecast, perhaps the best[260] method of transport for the future will be by sea.[270]   270 words

FACILITY DRILL FOR EXAMINATION PASSAGE 41:

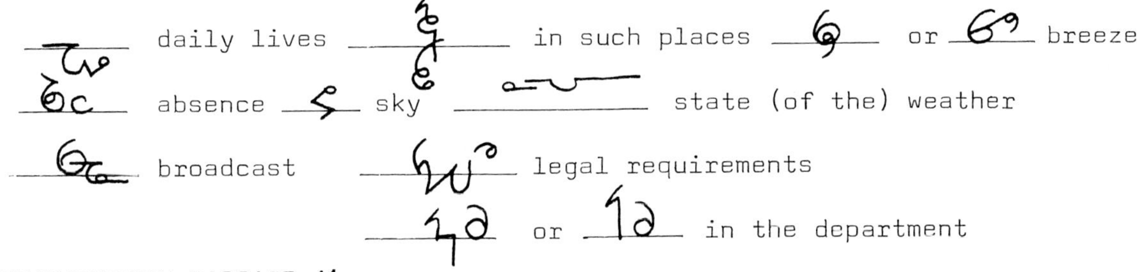

EXAMINATION PASSAGE 41:

Weather Forecasts (3 × 90)

The weather plays an important part in our lives. We[10] all know how much happier most people are when the[20] sun is shining, although this may not apply in countries[30] where it shines most of the time. In such places,[40] rain and a cool breeze are often a welcome relief[50] from the usual heat. The weather forecasts, too, have become[60] a regular feature of our daily lives, being broadcast on[70] radio and television and appearing in the news-papers. In fact,[80] in Britain one can dial a number and receive the[90] local weather forecast by telephone. One would hardly imagine that[100] the absence of these forecasts would have grounded all the[110] planes, as happened recently when there was a day's strike[120] in the department which produces them. It is apparently a[130] legal requirement that, before a plane takes off, the crew[140] must be informed of the state of the weather, so[150] without this necessary information, they were unable to begin their[160] journeys. In the days before radio and television, people had[170] their own methods of forecasting weather by studying the sky, [180] the growth of plants and the movements of animals and [190] birds.   There are many people who say that the forecasts [200] are more often wrong than right and, indeed, sometimes they [210] are so general as to be of little real value. [220]   Rain may fall in one place within a given area, [230] but miss another place nearby. In fact, where I live [240] it is common for rain clouds to circle all day, [250] without any rain actually falling. Yet, somehow, just having the [260] forecast seems to make the world a more predictable place. [270]

270 words

FACILITY DRILL FOR EXAMINATION PASSAGE 42:

______ or ______ cruel (Note ______ = cripple) ____________ some other

______ great pleasure ______ shredded ______ or ______ fascinating

______ taking up ______ captivity ______ once a day ______ assistant

EXAMINATION 42:

Keeping a Cage Bird (3 × 100)

It is often said that keeping birds in cages is [10] cruel and there is, no doubt, a lot to be [20] said for that point of view. However, it can also [30] be argued that, in many cases, caged birds have better [40] lives than they would have in the wild.   It all [50] depends on how well they are cared for, and the [60] following advice is offered to those who may be thinking [70] of taking up this very fascinating hobby.

First of all, [80] decide on the sort of bird you want to keep. [90] Some birds are extremely difficult to keep in captivity, so [100] it is best to start with one of the better-[110] known varieties. The next thing to consider is whether you [120] want to have just one bird or several. It is [130] obvious that the more birds you have, the more space [140] they will need, and it is asking for trouble to [150] put two birds into a cage which is designed for [160] only one. Ideally, even a single bird should have a [170] cage which is large enough to allow it to fly [180] around but where that is not possible, it should be [190] let out at least once a day and allowed to [200] fly about in the room. It is most important, of [210] course, that your bird is given the right kind of [230] food, but this is not a matter which presents any [240] great problem. Your local pet shop will probably stock several 250 kinds of bird seed and the shop assistant will be 260 able to help you to select the right one. Apart 270 from grain, it will probably require an occasional blade of 280 grass or some other vegetable matter, such as the shredded 290 leaf of a lettuce. If you look after your pet / properly it should give you great pleasure for many years. 300

300 words

FACILITY DRILL FOR EXAMINATION PASSAGE 43:

_______ great regret	_______ my decision	_______ this decision
_______ or _______ rosy	_______ of our policy	_______ company policy
_______ per annum _______ or _______ boardroom		_______ shut down
_______ level of production	_______ recent decision	
_______ one million dollars		

EXAMINATION PASSAGE 43:

Letter of Resignation (3 x 100)

Sir, It is with great regret that I ask you 10 to accept my resignation from the position of Marketing Manager. 20 I have no doubt that my decision will come as 30 a surprise to you and, as you can imagine, it 40 was not made before I had given the matter a 50 lot of serious thought. I also feel that you deserve 60 an explanation of how I reached this decision. When I 70 joined the company ten years ago, the outlook was far 80 from rosy. Although we had a good product, our factories 90 were working at a very low level of production and 100 we had many machines which were standing idle. We decided 110 that the answer to our problem was a policy aimed 120 at stimulating public demand for our product and I was 130 given the task of achieving that objective. Since then, turnover 140 has increased from under one million dollars per annum to 150 six million and I think I can claim some of 160 the credit for the success of our policy. Unfortunately recent 170 decisions taken at boardroom level will, in my opinion, lead 180 to a reduction in demand, and therefore, a fall in 190 production. As Marketing Manager, I was, of course, particularly upset 200 by last month's decision to reduce expenditure on advertising. I 210 cannot understand why the company is doing this at a 220 time when competition is

increasing. It is difficult to understand [230] why our small, but very successful, factory in Wellington should [240] have to be shut down. I can only conclude that [250] these two decisions are the result of a radical change [260] in company policy but it is a change which I [270] can neither comprehend or support. Therefore, I am sure you [280] will appreciate that, in the circumstances, the only course open [290] to me is regretfully to tender my resignation. Yours sincerely. [300]
<u>300 words</u>

FACILITY DRILL FOR EXAMINATION PASSAGE 44:

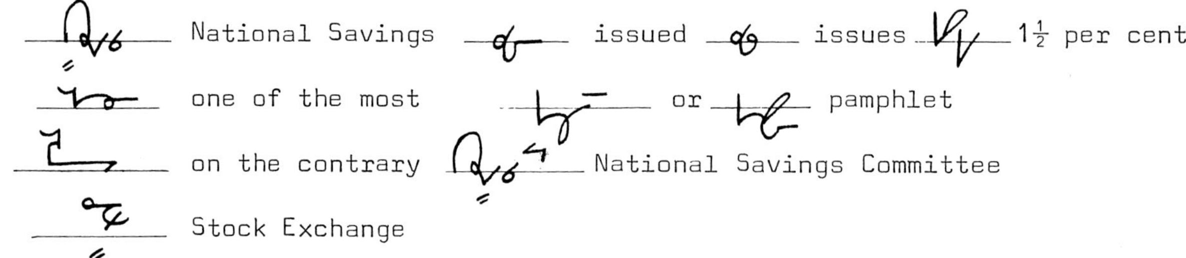

EXAMINATION PASSAGE 44:

<u>Investing Money</u> (3 × 110)

It is a good thing from time to time for [10] investors to take a look at the money they have [20] put into National Savings. Some of it may not be [30] earning the interest or increasing at the rate it could [40] be if it were invested elsewhere. This is particularly true [50] of those National Savings Certificates which were first issued a [60] great many years ago in the First World War. Many [70] of these earlier issues are now growing at a rate [80] well below the level of the present issues. For example, [90] those who have not cashed Certificates issued in nineteen-sixteen [100] are getting less than one and a half per cent [110] return. With prices rising at much more than this rate [120] in recent years, owners of these Certificates are just losing [130] money. Oddly enough, the National Savings Committee does not seem [140] to go out of its way to tell the holders [150] of these old Certificates that they would do much better [160] if they cashed them and re-invested the money in the [170] latest issue. On the contrary, the pamphlet which they print [180] tells people that there is no need to do this, [190] as the Certificates they possess will continue to earn interest, [200] however old they may be. This advice is of little [210] benefit to the individual whose savings are being swallowed up [220] by rising inflation.

Some of the earlier issues are certainly 230/ worth retaining but, in recent years, people have become interested 240/ in finding other ways of putting their capital to work. 250/ One of the most popular is to invest it with 260/ a building society, and the larger ones are usually safe 270/ and very strong financially. For younger people too, saving with 280/ a building society has advantages if they are intending to 290/ buy their own home, as they will have a much 300/ better chance of being granted a mortgage when that time 310/ comes. Stock Exchange dealings, however, are too risky to be 320/ indulged in by small savers, who might well lose everything. 330/   330 words

<u>FACILITY DRILL FOR EXAMINATION PASSAGE 45</u>:

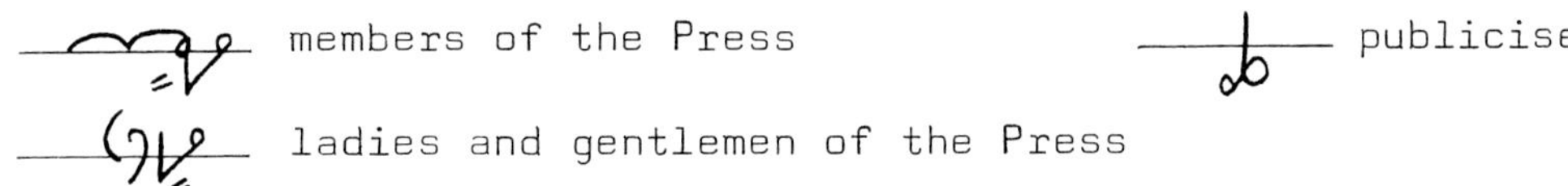

members of the Press   publicise

ladies and gentlemen of the Press

<u>EXAMINATION PASSAGE 45</u>:

<u>The Power of the Press</u> (3 × 110)

Ladies and gentlemen, This meeting has been arranged so that 10/ we can publicise the plans for our second factory, but 20/ before we get down to details, I would like to 30/ explain why I am so very pleased to see several 40/ newspaper reporters here this afternoon. It has always been the 50/ policy of this company to encourage members of the Press 60/ to take a close interest in our affairs. Years ago, 70/ when the company was trying to establish itself in this 80/ area, we met a lot of opposition from people who 90/ feared that our factory would turn out to be only 100/ the first of many. They were worried that the rural 110/ character of the area would be completely spoiled. We decided 120/ that the best way to overcome those objections was through 130/ the medium of the Press. We approached the editor of 140/ the local newspaper, who agreed to publish a series of 150/ articles, written by members of his staff, about the economic 160/ prospects of the area. In those days, if I remember 170/ correctly, seventy per cent of local workers were employed in 180/ farming and there was very little in the way of 190/ alternative employment. The series of articles created a great deal 200/ of interest, which was just what we wanted. Many of 210/ those people who had opposed the new factory changed their[220] minds when they realised that it would make a big[230] contribution to the future prosperity of the area. The fact[240] that our company was able to establish itself in this[250] part of the country was due, in no small part,[260] to the co-operation which we received from the ladies and[270] gentlemen of the Press, and that is why I am[280] particularly pleased to welcome them to this meeting. I am[290] sure they will find much to interest them during the[300] next few hours and that when they write their reports[310] they will show the same understanding of the needs of[320] this area as their colleagues did in those early days.[330]

330 words

FACILITY DRILL FOR EXAMINATION PASSAGE 46 :

no need   shoulders   specialists

EXAMINATION PASSAGE 46:

Opening a Bank Account (3 × 120)

It is worth while opening a bank account today because[10] of the many valuable services offered to you. If you[20] open a current account you will be given a cheque[30] book. Money deposited in this way earns no interest, but[40] it enables you to pay your bills by cheque. The[50] most obvious advantage of carrying a cheque book is that[60] there is no need to carry large sums of money[70] when you go on shopping expeditions. It gives you a[80] permanent record of payment if there is a query later[90] on. Some banks now have bankers' cards - an added service[100] by which you can cash cheques to a certain amount[110] at any of their branches. This carries a guarantee for[120] the shopkeeper that the cheque will be met within the[130] amount allowed. Then you can choose between having a deposit[140] account or a savings account. Both of these earn interest,[150] but a deposit account is intended for holding large sums[160] of money, which are not needed for immediate spending. A[170] savings account, on the other hand, enables you to accumulate[180] small sums. That type of account is suitable for children.[190] Married couples have joint accounts or separate accounts. There[200] are advantages both ways. Many banks suggest that while it[210] is useful for a husband and wife to have a[220] joint account, it is also a good idea for a[230] woman to have control over some money in her own[240] name. Banks can take a great deal of work off ^{250} your shoulders. Regular payments for sums of money can be ^{260} paid by them direct for many recurring expenses. For this ^{270} you will sign a banker's order. This informs the bank ^{280} how much to pay, how often and to whom. The ^{290} banks follows these through until they are either changed or ^{300} cancelled. Many people bank money all their lives without ever ^{310} meeting the bank manager. If you need advice on money ^{320} matters, you should pay him a visit. He has many ^{330} specialists round him to whom he can refer you, therefore, ^{340} his advice is sound and reliable. He can discuss with ^{350} you the advantages of different types of insurance or investments. ^{360}

<u>360 words</u>

FACILITY DRILL FOR EXAMINATION PASSAGE 47:

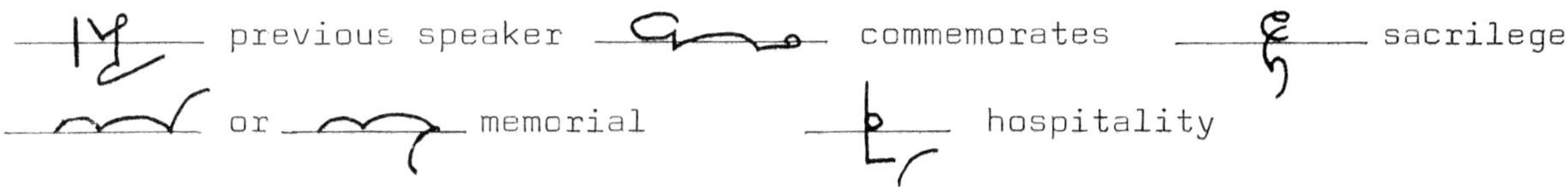

EXAMINATION PASSAGE 47:

<u>The Memorial Tree</u> (3 x 120)

Mr. Chairman, The previous speaker seems to think that this ^{10} is a matter of little importance which should not be ^{20} allowed to take up too much of our valuable time. ^{30} I must say I do not share her point of ^{40} view. The argument is not simply about a single tree ^{50} which may or may not be cut down; it is ^{60} about people's attitudes to the whole subject of the environment. ^{70} In these days, responsible people all over the world are ^{80} showing a great deal of concern over the way in ^{90} which the environment is being altered, and sometimes destroyed, in ^{100} the name of progress. It may seem to the previous ^{110} speaker that I am making much ado about nothing but, ^{120} in my opinion, the principles involved in trying to save ^{130} this solitary tree are exactly the same as those involved ^{140} in trying to save an entire forest. However, there are ^{150} particular reasons why this tree should be allowed to remain ^{160} where it has stood for more than one hundred years ^{170} and, with your permission, Mr. Chairman, I should like to ^{180} bring some of them to the attention of the members ^{190} of the audience. As you all know, the tree stands ^{200} on a small patch of grass behind the war memorial, ^{210} which commemorates the men of this village who gave their ^{220} lives in the Second World War.

In fact, although the^230 tree was already there when the memorial was erected, it^240 is considered to be part of the memorial. It is^250 actually known in the village as 'The Memorial Tree'. It^260 would surely be an act of sacrilege to chop it^270 down. Secondly, the tree is a landmark. It towers over^280 the war memorial and can be seen from the very^290 outskirts of the village. More than any other single thing^300 it makes our village different from the other villages in^310 this district. Finally, may I make a plea on behalf^320 of the great variety of birds who build their nests^330 in that tree every spring and whose songs give such^340 pleasure to so many people throughout the summer. Let us^350 continue to offer them the hospitality of our memorial tree.^360

360 words

FACILITY DRILL FOR EXAMINATION PASSAGE 48:

strange thing   arrive   time on their hands

EXAMINATION PASSAGE 48:

Strange Facts about Time (3 × 130)

Time is a strange thing. If one is waiting for^10 a friend to turn up or a train to arrive,^20 even a few minutes can seem a very long time,^30 but if one is hurrying to meet someone, or to^40 catch a train, the same few minutes seem to pass^50 with increased speed. If one is well and enjoying a^60 game or a walk, then an afternoon or an evening^70 quickly passes. If one is ill or in pain, the^80 same period of time drags very slowly by. Children usually^90 find it hard to wait for a few days for^100 a special event like Christmas or a birthday, but as^110 people get older, the years seem to spin past, each^120 one apparently shorter than the last.

Most people find that^130 time passes quickly when they are busy and would probably^140 prefer to have plenty of work than to have time^150 on their hands. It is a sad fact that once^160 people retire from work, a great many become ill with^170 boredom although they may often have longed for the day^180 to come when they did not have to go to^190 work any more. Today, many schemes are in operation which^200 prepare people for retirement, so that when it arrives, they^210 do not find time hanging heavily on their hands. Some^220 people never have enough time to do all they would^230 like to be doing, and usually they are healthier and^{240} happier than those who never know how to fill their^{250} days.

Another strange fact is that whenever someone is required^{260} to do a job, it is usually a busy person^{270} who agrees to take it on.

It has been said^{280} that work expands to fill the time available for it^{290} and this is often true. If I have a whole^{300} morning in which to clean, I find myself taking longer^{310} to complete the task. If I have several other things^{320} to do, I get through the cleaning in less time.^{330} Probably it is less thoroughly done, but the fact remains^{340} that it takes less time, because there is less time^{350} available and, maybe for that reason, I also work faster.^{360} I sometimes wonder what would happen if we had no^{370} way of knowing what time it was. Would our present^{380} life style change completely, or would it remain the same?^{390}

390 words

FACILITY DRILL FOR EXAMINATION PASSAGE 49 :

someone else's   motorbike   midnight

next door   boon   shift   disturbance

EXAMINATION PASSAGE 49 :

Noise (3 x 130)

How does one define noise? One person's noise may be^{10} someone else's music.

Most of the noises people complain about^{20} are quite legal, like the noise of a radio, or^{30} a motor-bike, and they may be enjoyed by the^{40} person who is causing them, but be annoying to someone^{50} else.

The law has to try to balance the right^{60} of one person to make a noise and the right^{70} of his neighbour to live in peace. If you live^{80} in a flat, you are bound to get some noise^{90} from a next-door or upstairs flat but, unless this^{100} noise is excessive, the law expects you to put up^{110} with it. Before you can make an official complaint about^{120} noise, it must be so bad as to interfere not^{130} only with your peace and comfort, but with the peace^{140} and comfort of any normal person living in that district.^{150} Even if it makes you ill, you will not be^{160} given any special consideration unless it is so bad that^{170} it would also make any ordinary, reasonable person ill.

If^{180} you live next door to someone who plays a musical^{190} instrument, the law would probably expect you to put up ^{200} with a certain amount of practising, but not for hours ^{210} on end, and certainly not during the night. In many ^{220} areas, there are local by-laws which exist to prevent ^{230} people from making a noise after midnight, so that if ^{240} someone is having a party and making a lot of ^{250} disturbance, the police can be sent for if it goes ^{260} on into the early hours of the morning. This is ^{270} not much comfort to those who have been kept awake ^{280} till then, especially if they have to get up very ^{290} early to go to work, but it is some help. ^{300}

There is a growing public concern about having radio channels ^{310} which operate for twenty-four hours each day.   This may ^{320} be a boon to shift workers or those who cannot ^{330} sleep, but I wonder how many others are kept awake ^{340} half the night by neighbours who have their radios on ^{350} too loudly. In my experience, people who are noisy tend ^{360} to be rather aggressive if anyone complains about them.   They ^{370} behave as if those who prefer peace and quiet are ^{380} in the wrong.

<u>383 words</u>

<u>FACILITY DRILL FOR EXAMINATION PASSAGE 50</u>:

______ of our company   ______ annual report   ______ take them as read

______ annual report and balance sheet   ______ for the accounts

______ history of the company   ______ Annual General Meeting

______ or ______ in particular   ______ in spite of the fact that

<u>EXAMINATION PASSAGE 50</u>:

<u>Annual General Meeting Report</u> (3 x 140)

Ladies and gentlemen, It is with very great pleasure that ^{10} I submit to you today the twenty-fourth annual report ^{20} and balance sheet of our company. These have been in ^{30} your hands for about ten days, and I hope you ^{40} will agree to take them as read. I am sure ^{50} you will regard the financial state of our company today ^{60} as highly satisfactory, especially when compared with the position last ^{70} year.

Some of you will be wondering why it has ^{80} taken so long for the accounts to be completed and ^{90} why our Annual General Meeting is being held a few ^{100} weeks later than is our custom. I must, therefore, explain ^{110} to you all that it is

owing to the expansion 120/ which has taken place during the past year.
I should 130/ like to draw your attention to the fact that, after 140/ having
carried out building operations in various parts of the 150/ country for almost
twenty-five years, we have, in the 160/ year just ended, built a larger number
of houses than 170/ in any previous year in the history of the company. 180/ Since
we first established our business, we have built about 190/ fifteen thousand
houses, which is a very large number. We 200/ think you will agree that this
is a very fine 210/ record to hold.
There are not many firms in business 220/ today who can equal it. One of the
reasons for 230/ our success is that we have been able to adapt 240/ ourselves to
the ever-changing requirements of the time. We 250/ have tried always to build
houses in which people could 260/ be happy.
The house in which people live is one 270/ of the most important factors affecting the life they lead. 280/ Our houses have stood the test of time and have 290/
won the approval of the public, who have been pleased 300/ to live in them. We
have also tried to build 310/ houses people could afford. Young couples, in
particular, want to 320/ feel they can meet the monthly repayments without too
much 330/ strain on their income, especially if the wife has, in 340/ time, to give
up her paid employment in order to 350/ have children and bring them up.
In spite of the 360/ fact that our building programme for last year was larger 370/
than in the previous year, you will notice that our 380/ net profits are
slightly lower. This is due partly to 390/ the high rate of tax imposed upon
us, partly 400/ because, to keep sales steady, we have not raised the 410/ prices
of our properties as much as we might have. 420/   <u>420 words</u>

<u>FACILITY DRILL FOR EXAMINATION PASSAGE 51</u>:

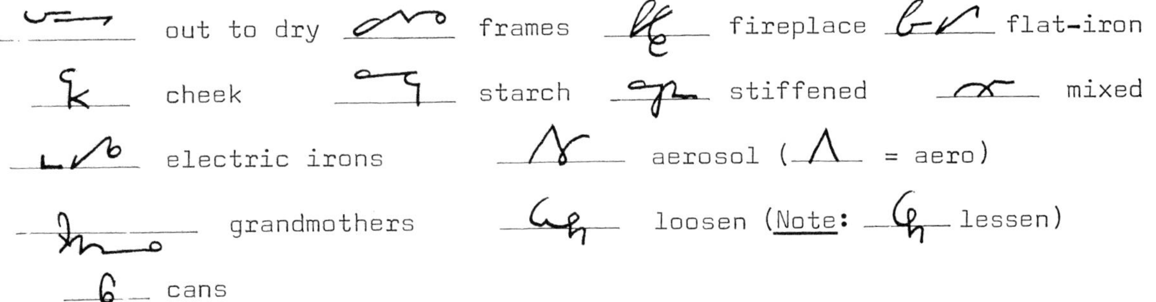

<u>EXAMINATION PASSAGE 51</u>:

<u>Wash-Day</u> (3 x 140)

When I was a child, washing clothes was a long 10/ and tiring business, so it was usual for one day 20/ to be set aside for the job, and in most 30/ households, it was Monday.   In those days, not many houses 40/ had any hot water supply, and so the first thing 50/ to be done was to heat the water, which was 60/ then poured into a larger container. Some of these were 70/ made of brick and had fires underneath, so that the 80/ water was heated inside them. Some were made of wood 90/ or metal, shaped like a tub, and the clothes were 100/ pounded with a specially-shaped stick to loosen the dirt. 110/

White clothes had to be separated from coloured ones, and 120/ were often boiled. You can imagine how much work was 130/ involved when all the rinsing water had to be heated, 140/ sometimes on an open fire.   Then the clothes would be 150/ put through a wringing machine, which had wooden rollers. These 160/ were moved by turning a handle at the side. Once 170/ the clothes were washed and rinsed, they would be hung 180/ out to dry, so if it rained on wash-day 190/ they were draped on wooden frames inside the house, round 200/ the fire place. Some houses had wooden racks which could 210/ be raised up by ropes and the clothes hung like 220/ flags from near the ceiling. When this happened, there was 230/ always a damp smell in the house. No-one liked 240/ wet wash-days.

Pressing was done on the kitchen table 250/ with a heavy metal flat-iron. These had to be 260/ heated, either on the open fire, or on top of 270/ a gas ring, and there were always two, so that 280/ as one was being used, the other was getting hot. 290/ The handles also got very hot, so they had to 300/ be held with a padded cloth.   Estimating the correct heat 310/ was done by holding the iron near the cheek - a 320/ rather dangerous method.

Items like shirts and cotton dresses, had 330/ to be stiffened with starch, so this had to be 340/ mixed ready for use before ironing them. However, as washing 350/ took so long, ironing was usually done the following day./ 360 Think how much easier it is today with washing machines, 370/ constant hot water on tap and electric irons, to say 380/ nothing of machines which spin clothes dry.
Modern clothing needs 390/ very little or no pressing, and if starch is used,/ 400

it comes ready prepared in aerosol cans.   Today's housewives may 410 not realise how lucky they are compared to their grandmothers. 420   420 words

---

TEELINE EDUCATION LIMITED runs a 'round-the-year' speed examinations service for groups of six or more candidates. Speeds from 50 to 140 w.p.m. (in tens).

For details, write to: The Examinations Officer,
                              Teeline Education Ltd.,
                              128 Kent Road,
                              Mapperley,
                              Nottingham, NG3 6BS.

Keys to Revision Exercises

<u>REVISION EXERCISE 1</u> (Page 5)

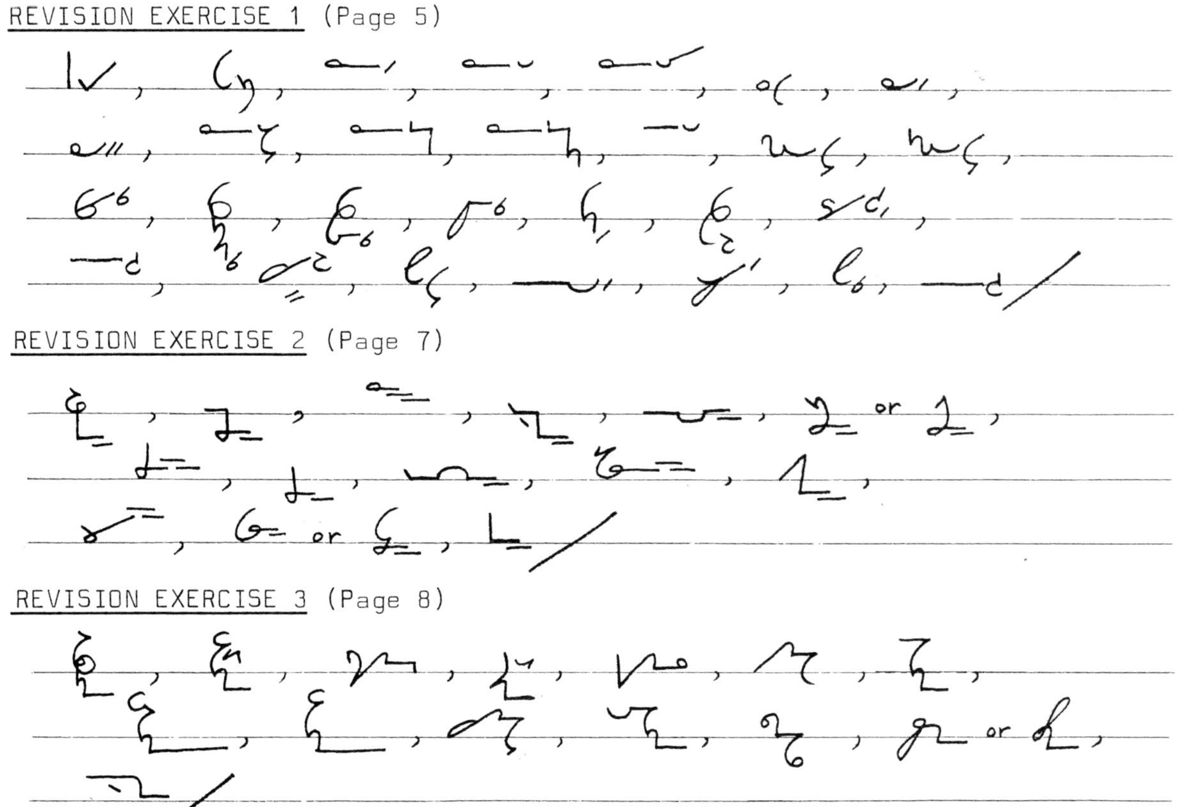

<u>REVISION EXERCISE 2</u> (Page 7)

<u>REVISION EXERCISE 3</u> (Page 8)